Tennyson: A Critical Study

Stephen Lucius Gwynn

Tennyson

A Critical Study

By

STEPHEN GWYNN

LONDON
BLACKIE & SON, Limited, 50 OLD BAILEY, E.C.
GLASGOW AND DUBLIN
1899

TO MY FATHER

Preface

For the existence of this book my pub-
lishers must be responsible. It seems to me
impossible to say anything that is at once
new and true about Tennyson. But, having
undertaken to write a critical study of him, it
seemed to me best to give, as clearly as I
could, my own point of view, and for that
reason I have abstained from extending my
knowledge of the many books which have
been written about him by admirable critics.
Contemporary criticism of his earlier poems
I have studied primarily for its historical
interest, and in the process of illustrating
it by quotations, I have had to expose my
own work to very damaging comparisons.

There is no more to be said here, but to
express my thanks to the Messrs. Macmillan
for their courteous permission to me to
illustrate my criticism by full quotation; to
Mr. Stephen Phillips for leave to reprint his

beautiful *Launcelot and Guinevere*, which has
hitherto only appeared in the columns of a
newspaper; to Mr. St. Loe Strachey for some
excellent suggestions; and chiefly to Mr.
G. H. Ely, not only for unwearying assistance
in the business of proof correction, but for
much valuable criticism of details.

STEPHEN GWYNN.

February, 1899.

Tennyson

A Critical Study

Chapter I.

Biographical.

In all cases criticism should bear some relation to biography; in many, the two are inseparable. Sometimes the events and external circumstances of a life intertwine themselves inextricably with a poet's work, as they did with Byron's; sometimes an alien influence can be detected, like a coloured liquid poured into water, traceable at first in its distinct hue, though materially in fusion, then gradually merging into a single but changed whole. So one can watch the first crude appearances of Godwin's teaching in Shelley's poetry, and follow the development till there is no separable Godwin, but a new Shelley. Tennyson's is the very opposite of such natures. The most significant thing about his biography is—if one can say so without disparagement—its lack of significance. You find there a most interesting book; you arrive at a picture of the man in his habit as he lived, and not only of him, but of the friends who surrounded him; but the story of his life is not unfolded, for the excellent reason that there was no story with dramatic episodes or mental turning-points for the biographer to tell.

You might as well try to write the biography of
an oak. It sprang in a good soil, it drew to itself
sustenance from the sap of earth and the dew of
heaven, it put out leaves and branches, it became
a stature in the forest; but there was no point at
which you could say, Something has happened.
That is a fair image, indeed Tennyson himself has
used it in one of the most characteristic among his
later poems. If you go to sum up his life, what
you find is this: That he was born in 1809, that he
was bred as a gentleman should be, that he wrote
poems, became laureate, grew rich through his art,
was the close and honoured friend of the men most
honourable in his time, and after eighty-four years
died, beautiful and majestic in his death. The
whole is a process of growth, gradual and stately,
but of events there are none. The only thing in
Tennyson's life which needs to be stated to explain
any of his poems is that he had a friend whom he
loved and looked up to; that this friend suddenly
died young, and that the poet enshrined his memory in perhaps the finest of all his verse. Nor is
there any trace distinguishable of any sudden ad-
mixture in his mind. He knew Carlyle intimately,
but you cannot put your finger on any poem and
say, Here Carlyle comes in. Yet there is no man
in all English literature more closely in touch with
the thought of his times. His mind was an ab-
sorbent; essentially a brooding mind,· that slowly
drew in to itself the vital elements out of the atmosphere which it breathed and converted them into
a definable shape. In a sense no poet is more
personal, more self-created; in a sense none more
impersonal, none more devoid of all eccentricities
and waywardnesses. He led, but it was always on
a path that his countrymen were already prone to
follow; he struck off at no abrupt tangents; and
whether in matters of religious faith, domestic re-

form, or imperial aspirations, he had the happy skill to formulate the thought that was lying vague and chaotic in the minds of millions, who instantly knew it and appropriated it to themselves. So typically and normally English is his poetry, and so completely was it assimilated by his contemporaries, that it is difficult to separate cause and effect, and say where he influenced, and where he was influenced by, the general feeling of his countrymen. Thus it is all but impossible to mark off particular moments in his life as important: for he hardly once seems to have come into collision with a popular prejudice or to have felt the even tenor of his way interrupted by any new motive or new impulsion. However, the first thing to be done is to sketch in outline the man himself, his life and his circumstances.

Alfred Tennyson was born on August 6th, 1809. His father, the Rev. George Clayton Tennyson, was the eldest son of a gentleman who owned a large landed estate, but in consequence of some caprice disinherited him in favour of a younger brother. As a compensation family livings in Lincolnshire were bestowed on him, and his home was the Rectory of Somersby. Thus Tennyson drew his origin directly from the two great conservative elements in English life: the church and the land. The Radicalism of his younger days was far less fundamentally characteristic of the man's whole nature than his later hostility to change. But whether as Radical or as Tory, he was always essentially an aristocrat.

There was a large family of them—eight sons and four daughters. Alfred Tennyson was the fourth child. He was sent to the neighbouring Grammar School at Louth when he was seven, but left it before he was twelve, and for the rest of his boyhood studied under his father. The education

was a singularly fortunate one, and consisted mainly
in allowing the boy to follow out the bent of his
own mind. From his earliest years Alfred Tennyson had shown the passion for verse-making; when
a mere child, his future was already fixed in his
own mind; he meant to be famous, and to be
famous as a poet. Everything about him tended
to encourage rather than to repress this instinctive
ambition—a circumstance of the utmost importance
with a nature so sensitive as his. But the Rectory
was in these days, what Johnson called Pembroke
College, "a nest of singing birds". The father
wrote verse with considerable skill; almost all of
the brothers and sisters did the same, and some of
them displayed a power that was above mere talent.
Thus there was a continual competition among
them, such as existed among the young Brontës,
and a general interchange of stories and poems.
Alfred, however, seems to have been recognized as
the leading spirit, for his father is said to have re-
marked: "If Alfred die, one of our greatest poets
will have gone". The boy was then only fourteen, but he was already the author of innumerable
poems; including "an epic of six thousand lines
à la Walter Scott", and a blank-verse drama, of
which some curious fragments are published in the
Life. These early productions are chiefly interesting as showing his taste in poetry; Thomson's
verse was one of the earliest models; then came
Pope's turn; Byron was a passion; and as early as
his twelfth year one finds him writing an elaborate
criticism of the *Samson Agonistes* in a letter to his
aunt—a delightful example of infant precocity with
its solemn commendation of the various excellences.
Another poem, "The Coach of Death", of the same
period shows unmistakable traces of the *Ancient
Mariner*. For the final fruits of this period of
discipleship one must look to the *Poems by Two*

Brothers, which Charles and Alfred induced Jackson
of Louth to publish in 1827; Frederick Tennyson,
the eldest brother, also contributing.

Thus it was after a boyhood spent almost entirely
at home, and devoted almost exclusively to the pursuit of poetry, that Tennyson went up to Cambridge
in February, 1828, when he and his brother Charles
matriculated together at Trinity College. They
came up with few acquaintances and no particular
academic distinction; but the way was no doubt
smoothed for them by Frederick Tennyson, who
had been captain of Eton, and was now a University prizeman; and most of all by Alfred Tennyson's personal appearance. To the extraordinary
and impressive beauty of his head was added great
dignity of stature and great bodily strength. "I remember him well," writes FitzGerald, who did not
know him till later, "a sort of Hyperion." His life
at Cambridge was undoubtedly formative; yet the
influence of Cambridge on Tennyson is not nearly
so unmistakable as the mark set by Tennyson on
Cambridge. He was recognized there at least ten
years before he was generally known in London,
and he became the object of a cult to the ablest men
of his day, who preached his poetry *urbi et orbi*
like a gospel. But Cambridge for him meant not
so much the recognized authorities of the place as
its stones and trees, it meant especially the personal
associates of his own standing. University honours
he never sought, and in 1831 he went down without
taking a degree. For the Chancellor's prize he
only competed under pressure of his friends' exhor-
tations, and *Timbuctoo* was merely an old poem
modified to suit the occasion. But he became a
part of the brilliant group among whom Spedding,
Milnes (Lord Houghton), and Trench were leading
figures, and whose natural leader was Arthur Hallam, son of the historian. To Tennyson was con-

ceded a rank apart in the informal Essay Club
which they called the Apostles.   He appears to
have been less of a disputant than the rest, and by
common consent was absolved from the duty of
writing papers.   His presence was taken to be a
sufficient contribution, and he went quietly on his
own way, absorbing rather than promulgating ideas,
but nevertheless looked up to not less than Hallam.
Between these two young men, by general consent
the most notable figures of a notable group, grew
up the closest friendship, which gained a fresh link
in 1829 when Hallam became engaged to Miss
Emily Tennyson.

The record of the friendship is written in imperishable verse, and the biography adds little to
our knowledge of it.   Tennyson's letters to his
friend were destroyed by Henry Hallam after his
son's death, and of Hallam's to Tennyson few are
printed.   Yet these bear out the impression left by
the poem that the poet's relation to his friend was
one of deference.   Hallam was not merely the literary
confidant, but also the spiritual counsellor; for at
this period Tennyson was much preoccupied with
religious doubts, which, in themselves harassing,
afflicted him the more as seeming to separate him
finally from his own folk, all of whom held to the
orthodox faith, and some even to a rigid Calvinism.
Hallam shared the doubts, but his nature was
sanguine and free from the morbid strain never
wholly absent from Tennyson, and dominant in his
youth.   In the course of his life Tennyson took
counsel with many men, but only this one seems
to have exercised a moral ascendency over him.

Hallam, on his part, was among the most fervent
in his anticipations of greatness for his friend, who
so far outstripped him in the art to which he also
aspired.   In 1830, when Tennyson was under twenty-
two and still an undergraduate, the first volume of

Poems Chiefly Lyrical was published. The strongest eulogy was written by Hallam, who in this matter expressed the voice of Cambridge. Outside of the university little effect was produced by this book, though Christopher North reviewed it half-seriously, half-scoffing, and old Rogers predicted great things. In 1831 Mr. Tennyson, the father, died, and Alfred Tennyson left Cambridge to live at Somersby, where the family remained in occupation of the Rectory, renting it from the new incumbent. But there was no break in the ties with the Cambridge group, which were maintained actively by visits and correspondence. In the end of 1832 appeared the second volume of poems, containing *The Lady of Shalott*, *The Lotos Eaters* (in its early form), *Œnone*, and *The Palace of Art*—in short, giving to the world earnest and not mere promise. The poet's name was now of sufficient mark for him to be made the subject of an article in the *Quarterly*, written by the bitter pen of Lockhart. But there was plenty of commendation in other reviews, and the Cambridge Union fell to debating whether Tennyson or Milton were the greater poet. The value of this enthusiastic backing from his own university was inestimable to a poet so acutely sensitive to hostile criticism as it was Tennyson's misfortune to be. But the main support was Hallam's sympathy, and that support was soon to be taken away. The two had been incessantly together, not only in Cambridge, but abroad. In 1831 a wild enterprise took them to Spain to support the Spanish insurgents under General Torrijos against the despotism of Ferdinand; they came back without adventures—none, at least, are recorded—but with plentiful inspiration from the Pyrenean gorges and torrents in the valley of Cauteretz, where *Œnone* was in part written.

When Tennyson settled down at Somersby

Hallam started his career in London, actively at
work on magazine articles; but in the following
summer he and Tennyson again went abroad, this
time to the Rhine. In 1833 Hallam again set out
for the Continent in company with his father, and
after a final evening in Hallam's rooms the friends
parted for the last time. Arthur Hallam died suddenly at Vienna on September 15th, 1833. The
news was communicated to Tennyson, who beyond
his own sorrow had the agony of breaking it to his
sister. Her long illness which followed helped to
blacken the world to her brother, yet her need for
comfort gave a purpose to his life, which, for some
time at least, "crept on a broken wing". He was
haunted by fears of blindness, and actually suffered
a great deal from his eyes; the reception of his
poems discouraged him; he thought of writing no
more, and even, as it would seem, meditated the
question of suicide. His poem *The Two Voices*
reflects the debate that was in him at this period;
the far nobler work *Ulysses* expresses his reaction
against despair. Already stray stanzas and cantos
of the *In Memoriam* had taken shape, but no
finished whole was projected. He lived on at
Somersby, sharing the daily life of his mother
and sisters, much hampered by lack of money, but
in close touch with the things that in very large
degree constituted his early inspiration—the breath-
ing nature about him and the rough homeliness of
Lincolnshire folk.

He was determined to publish no more till he
could give the world of his best, and in the ten
years between 1832 and 1842 he was assiduously
at work pruning and amending his earlier work
and composing new. Also about 1837 a new factor
entered into his existence. He became engaged,
more or less formally, to Miss Emily Sellwood,
whom he had first met in 1830, a beautiful girl of

seventeen, sister to the wife of his brother Charles. The engagement and their correspondence lasted till 1840, when it was broken off with no prospect of marriage ever ensuing. The stimulus which would have driven another man to seek employment and money wherever it could be found, even in the merest hack-work, did not turn Tennyson from his purpose. He was even unwilling to allow publication of his finished work in magazines, and as for what had been already published, he deprecated all public criticism of it. Nothing, not even his desire for the woman he had chosen, interfered with what he conceived to be the necessity of his art. So there came a separation between the lovers which lasted over a silence of ten years. In the meantime the household of which Tennyson was now the head had been torn up from its roots in Somersby. In 1837 they left the Rectory and migrated first to Tunbridge Wells, then to Boxley, near Maidstone. This brought the poet nearer to London, and his visits were frequent enough to the friends of his own generation and to those of an older standing, from Rogers to Carlyle. These were the days of tavern dinners, such as are celebrated in *Will Waterproof*, and it was at this period that Carlyle etched one of his inimitable portraits in a letter to Emerson.

" Alfred is one of the few British and foreign figures (a not increasing number, I think) who are and remain beautiful to me, a true human soul, or some authentic approximation thereto, to whom your own soul can say 'Brother'. However, I doubt he will not come [to see me]; he often skips me, in these brief visits to town; skips everybody, indeed; being a man solitary and sad, as certain men are, dwelling in an element of gloom, carrying a bit of Chaos about him, in short, which he is manufacturing into Cosmos. . . . He had his breeding at Cambridge, as if for the Law or Church; being master

of a small annuity on his father's decease, he preferred
clubbing with his mother and some sisters, to live un-
promoted and write Poems.   In this way he lives still,
now here, now there; the family always within reach of
London, never in it; he himself making rare and brief
visits, lodging in some old comrade's rooms.   I think
he must be under forty, not much under it.   One of the
finest-looking men in the world.   A great shock of
rough dusky dark hair; bright, laughing, hazel eyes;
massive aquiline face, massive yet most delicate; of
sallow brown complexion, almost Indian looking, clothes
cynically loose, free-and-easy, smokes infinite tobacco.
His voice is musical, metallic, fit for loud laughter and
piercing wail, and all that may lie between; speech and
speculation free and plenteous; I do not meet in these
late decades such company over a pipe! we shall see
what he will grow to."

Carlyle's advice to Tennyson is notable as one
of the few positive recommendations laid down by
that sage.   It was to the effect that he should leave
verse and rhyme and apply his genius to prose—a
singularly unwise exhortation, as the volume published in 1842 was soon to prove.   This contained
among the new poems *Locksley Hall* and the *Morte
d'Arthur*; but the main character of the additions
was given by the English Idyls, *Dora*, *The Gardener's Daughter*, and the rest.   His fame may be
dated definitely from the publication of this volume.
Posterity, someone has said, commences at the
frontier; and his work was widely read and criticised outside of this country.   At home Oxford was
now scarcely less enthusiastic than Cambridge, and
Carlyle wrote the "true deposition of a volunteer
witness", in a wonderful letter of gratitude.   Still
there were many harassing circumstances in his
existence.   All his own private fortune, which had
hitherto yielded a small income, and a portion of
that belonging to his brothers and sisters, was

invested in a manufactory for turning out wood-carvings, and the whole was lost. But his brother-in-law insured the life of Dr. Allen, the company promoter, in Tennyson's interest, and this gentle-man very opportunely died in the following year. Luck now turned. In 1845, at the instance of Monckton Milnes (Lord Houghton), Peel granted a pension of £200 a year; the argument used was, it is said, a reading of *Ulysses*. In 1847 *The Princess* appeared, in which Tennyson with his usual tact gave a direction to the thoughts upon woman's position then occupying the popular mind. In 1850 came *In Memoriam*, and the poet at once stepped into the position which became increasingly imposed upon him, of religious teacher outside the pale of dogma. This year marks the turning-point in his life. In the spring he met Miss Sellwood after a separation of ten years; and he felt that his means were now sufficient to offer her a home. They were married on June 13th—he aged 41, she 37—and it seems clear that he never said a truer thing than the utterance quoted by his son, "The peace of God came into my life before the altar when I wedded her". In the following November came the offer of the laureateship; and from this onward the *Life* is nothing but the un-broken record of a series of successes.

One misfortune came at the outset: his first child, a boy, was born dead. On Mrs. Tennyson's recovery they went abroad, travelled in Italy, and met the Brownings. Returning to England in the close of 1851, they found the country in a high fever of anxiety about its defences, and Tennyson wrote the earliest of his national songs—*Britons guard your own* and *Hands all round*: but his strong feeling for the greatness of his race found a far nobler expression in his *Ode on the Death of the Duke of Wellington*—a magnificent poem which by some amazing error in popular judgment was received with almost universal condemnation. It was a new experience and an embittering one to his over-sensitive nature; but, conscious of his developed art, he went straight on his way. His personal concerns were prosperous; two sons were born to him in quick succession, and children always seem to have been to him a source of delight. In 1853 he felt justified in taking a lease of Farringford, the beautiful house in the Isle of Wight, with the option to purchase, and so he settled down into the home, and among the scenes, with which his memory will for ever be associated.

In December, 1854, *The Charge of the Light Brigade* was written, and the enthusiasm which it aroused among the soldiers in the Crimea was such a reward as comes to few writers. A thousand copies were printed by Tennyson and circulated among the troops as a mark of his gratitude for their welcome to the verse. In 1855 came *Maud*, and at this distance of time it is difficult to account for the storm which that poem roused. To the end of his days Tennyson cherished a special affection for it, and for the Funeral Ode, which was probably born in part of the instinct to rise in defence of them. But the man who within five years had published *Maud* and *In Memoriam*, had no occasion to trouble about critics—though he did so. He had reached the climax of his genius; and though he wrote things later on, even up to the very slope of the grave, that may challenge comparison with the glow of his earlier poems, the concentrated force of *In Memoriam*, or the passion of *Maud*, his work from this onward began to decline.

Not that his contemporaries thought so. The first Idylls of the King, *Enid, Vivien, Elaine, Guinevere*, appeared in 1858, and were received "with tumult of acclaim". Whereas before it had often been the many, the average well-informed critics or reviews, who censured, and the few who applauded, it was now a general chorus of enthusiasm in which the most enthusiastic voices came from men like Thackeray and Gladstone. But at the same time, from certain among the faithful of old days,—notably from Ruskin and FitzGerald,—there came now a half-uttered protest—praise tempered with deprecation of the new departure. I shall have more to say of this later, but this is the place to note that Tennyson, becoming more exclusively a writer of picturesque description, and assuming more and more consciously a didactic purpose, drew further and further away from the real heart of life. From this onward there is really nothing to record. In 1873 the offer of a baronetcy was refused. In 1875 Tennyson embarked upon a new branch of literature, and published *Queen Mary*, which was played in the next year. *Harold* followed in 1877. *Becket*, though not published till 1884, was written by 1879, in which year *The Falcon* was produced by Mr. and Mrs. Kendal. Meanwhile the receipts from his poems had made this poet perhaps the richest man who ever earned his money by verse. His beautiful house of Aldworth was built (by Mr. James Knowles) on Blackdown among the Surrey Hills, but the Isle of Wight was still the home of his choice. In 1880 appeared the volume of *Ballads and other Poems* containing *Rizpah* and *The Revenge*, which rank with his best work. In the same year Sir Henry Irving and Miss Terry played in *The Cup*, and in 1882 Mrs. Bernard Beere brought out *The Promise of May*. 1883 saw his famous cruise in the *Pembroke Castle*, when Mr. Gladstone, then at the height of his reputation, scarcely attracted more attention than the poet. In the autumn of this year a peerage was offered him, and after some hesitation was accepted. In 1885

came the volume entitled *Tiresias*, stamped with
that increasing preoccupation in religious subjects
which marks his later work.   Yet none of the poems
in it which concern men's position in the universe,
or that belief in the soul's imperishable nature
which seemed to Tennyson the most vital of all
faiths, are so likely to live as the eulogy of Virgil
—perhaps his very finest technical achievement—
which appeared in this volume.   In 1886 came a
great sorrow, the death of his son Lionel, who suc-
cumbed to Indian fever while on his way home-
ward, and was buried in the Red Sea.   His
memory is enshrined in the volume issued in 1887
not only in the poem *Locksley Hall Sixty Years
After*, but in the dedication to Lord Dufferin, a
noble expression of the dignified grief that does not
overpower gratitude.   The title poem marks fitly
enough all the change that had come in the poet's
mental development; but while all the beliefs of
youth, all the enthusiasm for progress, had faded
into a deeper sense of man's petty station in the
universe, and into a less confident historical survey
which saw not only the flow but the inevitable ebb
in all human effort, yet there was present a more
assured conviction, a more nourished hope, that the
single human existence was only a beginning or a
stage, and in no sense a blank end.   In 1888 came
the poet's first serious illness; yet he rallied, and in
1889 published still one more volume, containing
the poem *Crossing the Bar*, which his son not un-
fitly calls " the crown of his life's work ".   In 1892
his play *The Foresters* was produced in America;
that was among his latest interests.   His final illness began early in September, though he had felt
the end approaching long before. His great strength
kept him living for a month, and death, when it
came, was a slow ebbing of life.   The actual circumstances of the scene are described with great

tenderness and beauty by his son in a passage that
I do not care to mutilate by imperfect quotation.
The final words of it may be borrowed:—

"Some friends and the servants came to see him.
He looked very grand and peaceful, with the deep
furrows of thought almost smoothed away; and the old
clergyman of Lurgashall stood by the bed with his
hands raised and said, 'Lord Tennyson, God has taken
you, who made you a prince of men! Farewell.'"[1]

That phrase accurately renders the impression
made upon one by reading the *Life*. There is no
doubt that a biography written, as are most modern
biographies, from the point of view of a *valet de
chambre*, might have insisted on Tennyson's irrit-
able susceptibility to criticism and the frequent
brusqueness of his manner to strangers, probably
occasioned by sheer absence of mind. But unless
nearly all the people who have led the movement of
England in the last half-century were mistaken, the
great artist was also one of the most lovable among
men. I may quote for a final appreciation of him
this passage from a paper by Mr. Locker Lampson
given in the *Life*, which gains a special value from
the fact that the writer was delightfully alive to the
humours of the poet's eccentricities. He was not
afraid to laugh at Tennyson, but he was by his
own confession still better disposed to laugh with
him.

"Balzac's remark that 'Dans tout homme de génie
il y a un enfant' may find its illustration in Tennyson.
He is the only grown-up human being that I know of,
who habitually thinks aloud. His humour is of the
dryest, it is admirable. Did anybody ever make one
laugh more heartily than Alfred Tennyson? He tells a
story excellently, and has a catching laugh. There are
people who laugh because they are shy or disconcerted,

or for lack of ideas, or to bridge over some conversational gap or obstruction; only a few because they are happy or amused, or perhaps triumphant. Tennyson has an entirely natural and a very kindly laugh.

"I and mine have a very warm regard for Tennyson. He has been very kind to Mrs. Locker and me. The more we see of him, the more we appreciate his singular charm, which has never deserted him in this world, and which I trust will be secured to him in the next. His friendship has been, and still is, one of the solaces of my life."[1]

Chapter II.

Tennyson and Critical Opinion.

It has been shown that Tennyson's poetic faculty obtained prompt and enthusiastic recognition among a brilliant generation of Cambridge undergraduates. Beyond this circle, however, beyond the range which could be reached by the imposing qualities of his voice and presence, he only won his way slowly, and, after the fashion of genius, excited a good deal of hostility. Critics recognized in him a new thing, and to the average critic the new is always at first sight repellent. If we are to realize how Tennyson struck his contemporaries, we must form some conception of the literary standards of that time. In 1830 Shelley, Keats, and Byron were dead; Wordsworth had long settled down into the mechanical dulness of *Ecclesiastical Sonnets*, and while he retained a surprising share of veneration, produced nothing to stimulate enthusiasm. Coleridge was rhapsodizing at Highgate, the living sepulchre of a "*poète mort jeune à qui l'homme survit*". Moore was brilliant as ever, but the trickle of his genuine though trivial inspiration had run dry; he was merely the successful man of letters, the quick-witted satirist, no longer the national singer. What the popular taste had sunk to in poetry may be inferred from Macaulay's onslaught in 1830, published in the *Edinburgh Review*, upon Robert Montgomery. Macaulay dealt widely in charges of puffery, but everybody who has written reviews knows very well that it is perfectly impossible to make the public read and buy anything that they do not honestly like. In default of a better they took Robert Montgomery to their hearts. How blank was the next decade, except for the advent of Tennyson, may be gathered by a study of the literary articles in the great Whig review, which represented probably the best and most temperate critical opinion of the day. In March, 1831, an article was devoted nominally to the poems of Mr. Edmund Reade,—which, to judge from the extracts given, would not obtain six lines of notice in any self-respecting paper to-day,—but really to a consideration of the state of contemporary poetry, and from it I shall quote largely. The article began:

"Perhaps there has never been a time since the prosaic days of Whitehead and Hayley in which so little good poetry has been issued from the press, as during the last two years. That some meritorious poems have been published within this period we do not deny, but we think that even they who look with partially indulgent eyes on the efforts of contemporary poets, will scarcely venture to affirm that any poetical works have lately appeared which have made much impression on the public taste, or have the slightest prospect of permanent popularity."

This, be it remembered, was written nearly a year after the issue of Tennyson's first volume.

"Yet with the exception of one or two great names,

we still possess all those eminent writers who have made
the first twenty years of this century as distinguished in
the annals of our poetry as the days of Elizabeth and
Anne. Scott, Moore, Southey, Wordsworth, Coleridge,
Campbell, Crabbe, Milman, Rogers, Bowles, and others
whom the recollection of our readers can easily supply,
are still living amongst us, and in the full enjoyment of
their poetical powers."

(It will be seen that Milman, Rogers, and Bowles
are classed by implication with Wordsworth and
Coleridge.)

"But they write no poetry; and, what is perhaps
stranger,—we do not expect it. We are content, even
when fresh from the re-perusal of their former poems,
to receive from their hands only prose; and 'prose by
a poet', instead of being an object of foolish and dis-
trustful wonder, is now almost the one thing sought.
Whence, we may ask, does this arise, at a time when
the activity of the public press exceeds all that has been
known in this or any other country—when education is
more diffused—the thirst for information greater—and
the means to satisfy it more abundant than perhaps at
any former period of our literary history? Various
causes may be assigned for this phenomenon. It may
be said that an excess of poetry, and an abundance of
that which was really excellent, has produced satiety
and fastidiousness. The public taste has been cloyed
with dainties, and over-excitement is succeeded by indifference. This may be true to some extent, but there
are other causes which have no reference to our recent
abundance of poetical treasure. The spirit of the age is
not eminently favourable to poetry. We say this not in
disparagement either of the spirit of the present age or
of poetry. Our observation is strictly compatible with
praise of both. The circumstance we have noticed arises
from the greater spread of knowledge and thirst for
information, and from a more just appreciation of the
powers of poetry and the relative place and importance

which it ought to occupy in literature. We now say more generally, as Horace did, 'Non satis est pulchra esse poemata, dulcia sunto'. We regard poetry not as our daily mental food, but as a sweet and costly fruit of which, though we derive from it greater pleasure, we partake more sparingly and less often, than of the homely prose which constitutes the staple aliment of our minds. We more judiciously assign to poetry that which is its peculiar office. We require not so much that it shall instruct as that it shall interest and delight us. We require that it shall appeal to our imagination and our feelings rather than to our judgment."

In short, for this gentleman grows long-winded, the day for didactic poetry was over. Nobody in 1830 would tolerate a poem like Grainger's *Sugar Cane*, with its minute instructions for the manufacture of rum. If a man had facts or theories to state he was expected to state them in prose.

"Towards mediocrity in poetry the public is becoming every day less tolerant. Few poems have a chance of being much read, unless their merits are of a very high order, or there is something strange, novel, and attractive in their subject. The public taste seems also to have decided that a poem must not be long. The pleasurable excitement which ought to arise from the perusal of poetry is, like that produced by music or painting, necessarily of short duration."

Now the first thing that strikes me on reading this diagnosis of contemporary taste is, that Tennyson from the very beginning was in touch with the popular demand. His early poems, whatever else they might be, were *dulcia*—even sugared. They appealed unquestionably to the imagination and feelings rather than to the judgment, and they were admirably short. The Edinburgh Reviewer had probably not heard of them; but the same could not be said after Lockhart had reviewed the 1832

volume in the *Quarterly*. There was no explicit
mention of it, however, between the buff-and-blue
covers, though Mrs. Norton, a very charming
woman but a very indifferent writer, was acclaimed
as "likely to attain an elevated place in poetry";
though Carlyle was allowed to eulogize Ebenezer
Elliott; and though a commendatory notice was
bestowed upon that very inoffensive person the
Rev. H. F. Lyte. Still, critical opinion was not
wholly blind to what was going on, and in January,
1836, we find an article which definitely recognizes
the existence of a new school of poetry at Cambridge. Town, says the reviewer, is no longer the
sole authority for the kingdom in matters of taste.

"Exclusive tribunals of public taste have fallen before
the spread of knowledge, and so have exclusive standards. While the lads of almost every public school in
England have been setting up their magazine, Cambridge, in addition to her critical and philosophical
journals, and her periodical Latin and Greek exercises,
has lately allowed a volume or more of juvenile English
poetry to struggle into daylight from under her maternal
wing."

Yet the new school, he continues, has nothing
academic about it; the classics are only one out of
many models; and from this point the reviewer
proceeds to discuss the models of the new school
with considerable judgment; although in reviewing
the early poems of Dean Alford, instead of Alfred
Tennyson's, he did undoubtedly, to borrow a
phrase from Lord Salisbury, put his money on the
wrong horse.

"A race which has shaken off the traditional yoke
of peremptory antiquity, could acknowledge, for some
brief interval only (and that unconsciously), a dictator
among immediate predecessors. It was natural, never-

theless, that the genius of Byron, which, during an interval of this sort, subdued nearly the whole poetical atmosphere of the country to its peculiar colour, should make a powerful impression on the youthful members of his own university. Kirke White came and went too soon to be affected by it. Indeed under any circumstances his gentleness and devoutness would have Byronized but ill. This spiritual domination, however, was one of those tyrannies which are now well-nigh overpast. The young poets whose common tastes and sympathies seem lately, at Cambridge, to be forming around them a little school, take as little after Byron as after Pope. They do not destroy the affections in the passions; they do not call on us to curse life, but to bless it altogether. Their light is not a concentrated glare whereby giants are to be shown, in attitudes of distorted greatness, forging thunderbolts which are to be hurled afterwards at their own bosoms. It is rather the gentle and kindly dawn of morning, doing little more than lift up the veil from nature, and spread out the world before us, that looking on it we may love it, and in some degree become like unto it. The poetry of Byron startled, and always must startle, every reader by its singularity and its power; nevertheless it has made mere imitators. It appears to have been too individual to become an element, developing, nourishing, and at last incorporating itself with other minds. It stands therefore by itself, a pyramid of black and dazzling marble—proud, monumental, barren; while all our poets of any really creative character, conscious of possessing, and determined to retain, their poetical identity, seem to be turning elsewhere for those assimilating and pervading qualities which are destined to feed them in their growth.

"Wordsworth says that he and his friends owe their poetical existence to Percy's *Reliques*—the ardent novices, of whom we are speaking, come apparently of the same descent; only one generation lower. For they derive directly from Cowper, Wordsworth, and Coleridge. These are the biddings to which their spirits are attuned, and their whole nature subjected. Singing, evidently, as the birds sing, for the very enjoyment of it, with some of them we are at times almost equally at a loss for the mere interpretation of their notes. Early youth appears to take peculiar pleasure in seeing language float along like an exhalation" [that is not a bad description of Tennyson's Juvenilia, *Claribel*, and the rest], "nor is it at that age the less liked, because in this condition it is a better medium for communicating colours than ideas. This defect has been encouraged by the schoolboy popularity of Shelley, whose language is often too yielding and aerial, of too delicate and gossamer-like a texture, to be the vehicle of so earthly a thing as substantial thought. Doubtless, Shelley always had his meaning; but it was not always as strong and definite a meaning as critics, intrusted with the rights of others, are bound to insist on having. Mr. Tennyson is perhaps at present the most known of any of the younger Cambridge poets who have taken wing. He must not set it down to acidity and moroseness if persons of riper years have regretted that his style was not sufficiently impregnated with thought; that more mind was not apparent behind his words. Mr. Alford appears to us to choose his subjects from a higher class, to conceive them with greater distinctness, and to have a stronger sense of the necessity of embodying his thoughts in precise expressions."

There is no doubt that the literary affinities of the new school are correctly traced in this interesting passage. Byron had exercised his "domination" over Tennyson's mind in boyhood; one can trace him on every second page in the *Poems by Two Brothers*; for instance, in this passage from a poem *On Sublimity*, where the discipleship to *Childe Harold* is obvious:—

> I love your voice, ye echoing winds, that sweep
>   Thro' the wide womb of midnight, when the veil
> Of darkness rests upon the mighty deep,
>   The labouring vessel and the shattered sail—
> Save when the forked bolts of lightning leap
>   On flashing pinions, and the mariner pale

Raises his eyes to heaven. Oh! who would sleep
　　What time the rushing of the angry gale
Is heard upon the waters? Hail, all hail,
Tempest and clouds and night and thunder's rending peal!

All hail, Sublimity! thou lofty one,
　　For thou dost walk upon the blast, and gird
Thy majesty with terrors, and thy throne
　　Is on the whirlwind, and thy voice is heard
In thunders and in shakings: thy delight
　　Is in the secret wood, the blasted heath
The ruin'd fortress and the dizzy height,
　　The grave, the ghastly charnel house of death,
In vaults, in cloisters, and in glowing piles,
Long corridors and towers and solitary aisles

But the real models, or rather influences, for
Tennyson found his own style earlier than most
poets, were Shelley and Coleridge. One can trace
definite resemblances to Coleridge, especially in an
early poem called *The Coach of Death* which is
printed in the *Life*, from which I quote the last
stanzas, where there is an unmistakable suggestion of *The Ancient Mariner.*

They pass'd (an inner spirit fed
　　Their ever-burning fires)
With a solemn burst of thrilling light
　　And a sound of stringed lyres.

With a silver sound the wheels went round,
　　The wheels of burning flame;
Of beryl and of amethyst
　　Was the spiritual frame.

Their steeds were strong exceedingly,
　　And rich was their attire:
Before them flow'd a fiery stream;
　　They broke the ground with hoofs of fire.

They glitter'd with a stedfast light,
　　The happy spirits within;
As stars they shone, in raiment white,
　　And free from taint of sin.

Shelley's mind rather than his manner influenced the young poet; perhaps indeed the affinity was more obvious to that generation than to us. At all events as late as 1839 we find an article in the *Edinburgh Review* complaining that Shelley's fame suffered from "the unbearable coxcombry of the 'intense' and mystical versifiers who made him their model—including both the Shellites of the old connection and those of the new, or Tennysonites". It will appear from this passage, even more strongly than from the review of Alford, that long before the 1842 volume, Tennyson was a perceptible force. Even the austere *Review* had recognized him, though grudgingly; in its notice of Lord Northampton's miscellany the *Tribute*, he is thrown into a list between Southey and Joanna Baillie, and pell-mell with Knight and G. P. R. James. The charge of obscurity, brought with touching regularity against any original poet at his appearance, is uppermost in the remarks upon the poem "Oh that 'twere possible"—the germ of *Maud* which Tennyson under compulsion from Monckton Milnes contributed to this volume.

"We do not profess perfectly to understand", says the reviewer, "the somewhat mysterious contribution of Mr. Alfred Tennyson entitled *Stanzas*, but amidst some quaintness and some occasional absurdities of expression, it is not difficult to detect the hand of a true poet—such as the author of *Mariana* and the *Lines on the Arabian Nights* undoubtedly is—in those stanzas which describe the appearance of a visionary form by which the writer is supposed to be haunted, amidst the streets of a crowded city."

It certainly was not difficult; and one would have thought that a critic might have seen that here was poetry worth a hundred *Marianas* and a wilderness of *Haroun Alraschids*. Reviewers no doubt were

many, though the *Review* was one; but considering
the editorial view of editorial responsibility in those
days one may not unfairly regard these criticisms
as the continuous utterances of a single tribunal,
and it is on that account surprising to find in a
review of Southey (Jan. 1839) the following remarks,
which practically repeat the complaint of 1831 that
poetry is torpid:—

"Even while many of our best poets are yet alive,
poetry herself is dead or entranced. It appears as if
the extraordinary physical discoveries of late years, by
throwing further and further back the boundaries of the
world of practical science and realizing the most visionary conceptions, had rendered cheap and vulgar the
wonders of imagination.   What are the subjects of
thought on which the minds of most men now love to
expend that surplus energy which is not absorbed by
the ordinary duties and exigencies of their station, the
favourite stuff of our daydreams?   The dominion attained by man over the elements, the wonderful changes
in commerce and communication, and all the relations
of life depending on them which are beginning to open
upon society.   These are topics which warm and exalt
the spirits, and render them peculiarly susceptible to
rhetorical exaggeration; but they are scarcely poetical.
Our fancies are bent on seeking sources of grandeur
and power, not in themselves and in the visionary world
which they can create, but in new and adventurous
combinations of external agencies; and to be recalled
from the latter to the former is, for the time, an interrup-
tion—almost an unwelcome one—to the course on which
they are so zealously set.   The star of the engineer, we
suspect, must be on the decline before that of the poet
can culminate again.   There is one train of thought
only, peculiarly remote from the affairs of the world,
and least of all disturbed by the whirl and noise of the
vast machinery about us in which sensitive minds now
peculiarly love to seek for refreshment — devotional
poetry is almost the only species cultivated with success.

"That this state of things is to last but for a time
the analogy of all past experience assures us.   Spirits
will arise which will so assimilate the mechanical temperament of the age to their own genius that it shall
furnish a new and rich fountain of poetry.   In the
meantime we are forced to content ourselves with re-
verting to the past and studying, as fairly as we are
able, the achievements of that school of which we have
seen the rise, progress, and decay within the remembrance of the living generation."

And so the reviewer proceeds to study as fairly
as he is able the great works of Southey.   From
the various extracts which we have made, two things
will appear.   First, that the influence of Tennyson's
early poetry was out of all proportion to its published bulk; he was recognized even by hostile
criticism as the head of a school—there were ad-
mittedly 'Tennysonites'—who had taken up, but
modified, the traditions of Shelley.   Secondly, that
a kingdom was standing vacant for the right man
to enter in upon it.   Tennyson did so with the
1842 volume.   And if one reads carefully the last
extract which I have quoted, it becomes more than
ever apparent how closely Tennyson was in touch
with the feelings of his time.   We may be still
looking, as Mr. Kipling's M'Andrew says, for
"another Robbie Burns to sing the song of steam",
but the poet who was able so "to assimilate the mechanical temperament of the age to his genius that
it should furnish a new and rich fountain of poetry";
—who found inspiration in "the dominion attained
by man over the elements and the wonderful
change in commerce and communication";—who
saw nothing adverse to poetry in the star of the
engineer—was no longer difficult to discover once
Locksley Hall was published; although, curiously
enough, it is one of the few poems not mentioned in
the *Edinburgh Review* article of April, 1843, which

made honourable amends for earlier neglect.   A
more remarkable conversion, however, was that of
the *Quarterly*.   In 1833 Lockhart took the 1832
volume and wrote a review of it, which goes far to
justify all that has ever been said by authors of
the malevolence of critics, or by critics of the uses
of the tomahawk.   Beginning with an ironical re-
traction of the attack upon Keats—tantamount to a
sneer at the stupidity of a public which, in spite of
common sense, indisputably admires such rubbish
as *Endymion*—Lockhart proceeds to recognize the
vogue which Tennyson's volume has attained, and
after an ironical compliment, quotes in ironical proof
of Tennyson's genius all the worst passages in the
book, upon which he fixes with the unerring instinct
of a born critic.   There are, for instance, extensive
extracts from a poem called the *Hesperides* which
is reprinted in the *Life*; a passage from *The Lotos-
Eaters* containing these lines—

> This is lovelier and sweeter,
> Men of Ithaca, this is meeter,
> In the hollow rosy vale to tarry
> Like a dreamy Lotos-eater—a delicious Lotos-eater;

and a full quotation of a somewhat maudlin though
pretty set of verses on *The Darling Room*, somewhat
in the manner of a more tuneful *Peter Bell*.   All
these things are taken and emphasized; so is also
one of the least felicitous sonnets—"Thine be the
strength of spirit fierce and free"—ever written by a
poet who never rose far above accomplished mediocrity in this form of verse.   In addition to this
detection of real flaws there is the cheapest kind of
ridicule heaped upon really beautiful passages in
The Lady of Shalott and *Œnone*, while for recognition of merit, which to so keen an eye must have
been everywhere apparent, we look in vain.   But
the review deserves not merely to be noticed, but

quoted, or pilloried, at some length. It opens thus:

"This is, as some of his marginal notes intimate, Mr. Tennyson's second appearance. By some strange chance we have never seen his first publication, which, if it at all resembles its younger brother, must be by this time so popular that any notice of it on our part would seem idle and presumptuous; but we gladly seize this opportunity of repairing an unintentional neglect, and of introducing to the admiration of our more sequestered readers a new prodigy of genius—another and a brighter star of that galaxy or *milky*-way of poetry of which the lamented Keats was the harbinger; and let us take this occasion to sing our palinode on the subject of *Endymion*. We certainly did not discover in that poem the same degree of merit that its more clear-sighted and prophetic admirers did. We did not foresee the unbounded popularity which has carried it through we know not how many editions; which has placed it on every table; and, what is still more unequivocal, familiarized it in every mouth. All this splendour of fame, however, though we had not the sagacity to anticipate, we have the candour to acknowledge; and we request that the publisher of the new and beautiful edition of Keats's *Works* now in the press, with graphic illustrations by Calcott and Turner, will do us the favour and the justice to notice our conversion in his prolegomena.

"Warned by our former mishap, wiser by experience, and improved, as we hope, in taste, we have to offer Mr. Tennyson our tribute of unmingled approbation, and it is very agreeable to us, as well as our readers, that our present task will be little more than the selection, for their delight, of a few specimens of Mr. Tennyson's singular genius, and the venturing to point out, now and then, the peculiar brilliancy of some of the gems that irradiate his poetical crown."

Here is a fair example of the way in which Lockhart pointed out beauties:—

"We pass by several songs, sonnets, and small

pieces, all of singular merit, to arrive at a class, we may call them, of three poems derived from mythological sources—*Œnone*, *The Hesperides*, and *The Lotos-Eaters*. But though the subjects are derived from classical antiquity, Mr. Tennyson treats them with so much originality that he makes them exclusively his own. Œnone, deserted by

> Beautiful Paris, evil-hearted Paris,

sings a kind of dying soliloquy addressed to Mount Ida, in a formula, which is sixteen times repeated in this short poem.

> Dear mother Ida, hearken ere I die.

She tells her 'dear mother Ida' that when evil-hearted Paris was about to judge between the three goddesses he hid her (Œnone) behind a rock, whence she had a full view of the naked beauties of the rivals which broke her heart.

> *Dear mother Ida, hearken ere I die.*
> It was the deep midnoon ; one silvery cloud
> Had *lost his way* among the pined hills:
> They came—*all three*—the Olympian goddesses,
> Naked they came—
>
> .   .   .   .
>
> How beautiful they were ; too beautiful
> To look upon ; but Paris was to me
> *More lovelier* than all the world besides ;
> *O mother Ida, hearken ere I die.*

In the place where we have indicated a pause follows a description, long, rich, and luscious—of the three naked goddesses? Fye for shame—no—of the 'lily flower violet-eyed' and the 'singing pine' and the 'over-wandering ivy and vine' and 'festoons' and 'gnarled boughs' and 'tree tops' and 'berries' and 'flowers' and all the *inanimate* beauties of the scene. It would be unjust to the *ingenuus pudor* of the author not to observe the art with which he has veiled this ticklish interview behind such luxuriant trellis-work, and it is obvious that it is for our special sakes he has

entered into these local details, because if there was
one thing which 'mother Ida' knew better than another, it must have been her own bushes and brakes.
We then have in detail the tempting speeches of, first:

> The imperial Olympian,
> With archèd eyebrow smiling sovranly,
> Full-eyèd Here;

secondly, of Pallas:

> Her clear and barèd limbs
> O'erthwarted with the brazen-headed spear;

and thirdly:

> Idalian Aphrodite ocean-born,
> Fresh as the foam, new-bathed in Paphian *wells*;

for one dip, or even three dips in one well, would not
have been enough on such an occasion—and her succinct
and prevailing promise of

> The fairest and most loving *wife* in Greece,

upon evil-hearted Paris's catching at which prize, the
tender and chaste Œnone exclaims her indignation
that she herself should not be considered fair enough,
since only yesterday her charms had struck awe into

> A wild and wanton pard,
> Eyed like the evening star, with playful tail;

and proceeds in this anti-Martineau rapture:

> *Most* loving is *she*.
> Ah me, my mountain shepherd, that my arms
> Were wound about thee and my hot lips prest
> Close—close to thine in that quickfalling dew
> Of *fruitful* kisses——
>
> Dear mother Ida, hearken ere I die.

After such reiterated assurances that she was about to
die on the spot, it appears that Œnone thought better

of it, and the poem concludes with her taking the wiser
course of going to town to consult her swain's sister,
Cassandra, whose advice prevailed upon her to live, as
we can, from other sources, assure our readers she did,
to a good old age."

That is the whole criticism of *Œnone*, and no
doubt the gentleman mentioned in the *Life* who
called the *Quarterly* "the best book in the world
next to God's own Bible" was convinced, with his
fellows, that *Œnone* was finally disposed of. It
serves Lockhart right to reprint after a lapse of
years this cheap and vulgar attempt to ridicule a
masterpiece. The same methods could be applied
with equal success to the balcony scene in *Romeo
and Juliet*, or to any other impassioned poetry; and
to the people who in the bottom of their hearts dislike poetry they would always be convincing. But
the extraordinary thing is that this man certainly
knew a great deal about poetry, and probably liked
it when the author was long dead and no longer
capable of exciting this exuberant flow of malevolence. For it will be observed that Tennyson
has justified the criticism by acting upon it.
Twenty-six lines of *Œnone* are quoted by Lockhart, and of these twenty have disappeared or been
altered, and the whole passage of "trellis-work" to
which he objected is removed.

The whole thing is the very quintessence of malice,
but admirable as destructive criticism. Tennyson
read it and was hurt to the very quick; but he
did not read it without profit. *The Hesperides*
disappeared from the reprint in 1843, so did the
verses on the room with its "two couches soft and
white"; so of course did the passage quoted in
The Lotos-Eaters, while the magnificent ending
was added; so did some verses quoted from *The
Lady of Shalott*, while others were altered. In

fact, out of all that Lockhart quoted not one line in
twenty is to be found in the 1842 edition.   Most
have disappeared altogether; many are altered; and
Tennyson has shown his own power of self-criticism,
under the bitter stimulus of Lockhart, both by what
he rejected and what he retained.   In vain did
Lockhart scoff at the sixteen-times-repeated refrain
of *Œnone*.   Tennyson knew when he was right
and could see when he was wrong.   Yet all the
fault-finding might have been done in a spirit that
would have done no hurt; as it was, the natural
morbid susceptibility of the man was aggravated
into a disease that never left him.

There is nothing further of much moment to
notice from 1842 onwards till we come to the publication of *Maud*.   Tennyson's position was assured,
even if he had not been appointed Laureate; but he
was still essentially the poet of the younger generation, and the following passage from Mr. Leslie
Stephen's *Studies of a Biographer* describes no
doubt rather the feelings of Oxford and Cambridge,
than the general verdict of England.

" Tennyson had already made his mark when I was a
schoolboy; and when I was at college all youths who
professed a literary turn knew the earlier poems by
heart.   Ebullient Byronism was a thing of the past.
There was no longer any need for the missionary zeal
which had taken Cambridge men of an earlier generation to propagate the worship of Shelley at Oxford.
'Chatter' about that luminary was already becoming
commonplace; a mere repetition of poetical orthodoxy.
Admiration of Browning, though it was distinctly beginning, implied a certain claim to esoteric appreciation.
But Tennyson's fame was established, and yet had not
lost the full bloom of novelty.   It was delightful to
catch a young man coming up from the country and
indoctrinate him by spouting *Locksley Hall* and *The
Lotos-Eaters*.   *In Memoriam* had just appeared when I

was a freshman—Tennyson became Poet Laureate in my first term—and *Maud* came out the year after I had graduated. . . . I only followed my companions when I tacitly assumed that 'poet' was a phrase equivalent to 'Tennyson'. The enthusiasm no doubt was partly obligatory; to repudiate it would have been to write oneself down an ass; but it was also warm and spontaneous. For that one owes a debt of gratitude to the poet not easily to be estimated. It is a blessing to share an enthusiasm, and I hope rather than believe that modern undergraduates have some equally wholesome stimulus of the kind."

Yet even in the midst of that enthusiastic admiration the appearance of *Maud* excited strong protests. In the *Edinburgh Review* it was treated fairly; due tribute was paid to the extraordinary beauty of the love passages; and the reviewer's very intelligent criticism of the metrical innovations which the poem contained will have to be discussed later; but there is a protest against the poet for being too much the child of his age, too much affected by the prevailing currents of thought upon political and social evils. But the general tone of the press may fairly be represented by Aytoun's review in *Blackwood*, concerning which that versatile person wrote to his publisher:—

"You know how I have stuck up for Alfred through thick and thin, and will readily believe that I have not come to this conclusion without a pang; but poetic justice must be done, else the small fry who are occasionally served up as whitebait for the gluttons of the Magazine, would have a just cause for complaint."

After expressing a sincere enthusiasm for the earlier poems, the critic owns to a distaste for *In Memoriam*, allows that he was disappointed with *The Princess*, and is now sadly convinced by the

perusal of *Maud* "that the man who has unquestionably occupied for years the first place among
the living British poets, is losing ground with each
successive effort". Aytoun then goes through the
poem, quoting with judicial impartiality passage
after passage, and denouncing their cacophony,
their namby-pamby sentiment, or their violence,
turn by turn. Two cantos only please him—that
beginning "A voice by the cedar tree" and "Come
into the garden, Maud". Here obviously we are
in presence of a critical opinion perfectly irrecon-
cilable with that which now obtains, and Aytoun's
objections are nearly all objections to qualities of
style. Tennyson's style must be considered elsewhere. It will suffice to say here that Aytoun sums
up his judgment of *Maud* by describing it as
"ill-considered, crude, tawdry, and objectionable".
And the oddest part of the matter is, that Aytoun's
sincerity is apparent in every line.

There was of course a vehement party of sup-
porters, and the fact that Tennyson received his
D.C.L. at Oxford in the year of *Maud's* publication
is significant. But it is worth while to examine
the utterances of a leading partisan in his faction to
see what precisely a devout Tennysonian admired
in Tennyson in the days when the master's fame
was still called in question. The essay published
in 1855 by George Brimley, a distinguished Cambridge scholar, may be taken as fully representative.
Brimley goes through the whole record of his
works from 1830 onwards. The earliest poems
seem to him, as they do to us, unreal and bodi-
less; some "are uninteresting from their subjects,
such as *The Merman* and *The Mermaid, The Sea-
Fairies, The Kraken, The Dying Swan*, &c. No
music of verse, no pictorial power, will enable a
reader to care for such creatures of the fancy." We
are more tolerant nowadays of the fancy, less cla-

morous for the human interest. *Mariana* and *The Arabian Nights*, in Brimley's judgment, stand out from the rest. In the second volume *The Miller's Daughter* and *The May Queen* "at once established Mr. Tennyson's capacity for becoming a popular poet and made him one within a limited circle". In the rest, Brimley complains, the work is like the work of a painter; it appeals to the sensuous and artistic perceptions rather than to the emotions. In short, Tennyson owed his early vogue rather to the domestic idyls than to *Œnone* or *The Lotos-Eaters*; indeed he recognizes this himself in *The Gleam*. "With the publication of the Third Series in 1842", Brimley continues, "Mr. Tennyson appears distinctly as the poet of his own age. . . . Mermen, mermaids, sea-fairies, Ladies of Shalott, lotos-eaters disappear from the scene; Adelines, Margarets, and Eleanores no longer come as abstract types of character without speech, story, or personal relations, figured forth in abundance of similes, but with none of the traits by which the mind apprehends individual men and women; Grecian nymphs no longer pour out their loves and griefs to their mother earth, and Grecian goddesses no longer interfere in the affairs of mortals and shed the lustre of celestial presences on the mountain side." Here is obviously again a critical standpoint very different from ours, which would rank *The Lady of Shalott*, *Œnone*, and *The Lotos-Eaters* among the poet's very best and most characteristic work, and certainly immeasurably higher than *Godiva* or *The Gardener's Daughter*, which are selected as masterpieces that can make "our human heart beat the stronger for reaction", and are not only constructed "to amuse the imagination". The desire for poems of English life and the quiet pathos of daily sights and scenes, which makes Brimley set a value to our eyes so disproportionate upon poems like *Dora* and *The Gardener's Daughter* is no doubt traceable to a reaction against that straining after the accidentally picturesque, which began with Scott's medievalism, ran into Byron's oriental scenes, and degenerated into *Lalla Rookhs* and their successors. Then follows a spirited defence of *Maud* and of *The Princess*, which latter poem is oddly described as one that "treats the sexual relations in their most comprehensive form, and may so be considered as containing implicitly all love poems as the poetical statement of the law which they all exhibit in particular instances". But Brimley's final eulogy is reserved for *In Memoriam* (as his final thrust is reserved for the critic in *Blackwood*, who "leaves it on the shelf with Blair's *Grave*"), and the last word of all appeals from the critics to the verdict of the people of England, who not only buy edition after edition, but have taken the New Year's hymn *Ring out, wild bells* for "a national song of hope and prophecy of all good things to come ".

In 1859 appeared the *Idylls*, and from this onward critical opinion resolved itself into a chorus of eulogy. The following letter from Thackeray is perhaps the extremest in expression, and also the most characteristic, of many letters of congratulation. It is written from an inn at Folkestone.

"My dear Alfred,

"I owe you a letter of happiness and thanks. Sir, about three weeks ago, when I was ill in bed, I read *The Idylls of the King*, and I thought 'Oh, I must write to him now for this pleasure, this delight, this splendour of happiness which I have been enjoying! But I should have blotted the sheets, 'tis ill writing on one's back. The letter full of gratitude never went as far as the post-office, and how comes it now?

"D'abord, a bottle of claret (the landlord of the

hotel asked me down to the cellar and treated me).
Then afterwards, sitting here, an old magazine, *Fraser's
Magazine*, 1850, and I come on a poem out of *The
Princess* which says, 'I hear the horns of Elfland blowing, blowing',—no, it's 'the horns of Elfland faintly
blowing' (I have been into my bedroom to fetch my
pen and it has made that blot),—and reading these
lines, which only one man in the world could write,
I thought about the other horns of Elfland blowing in
full strength, and Arthur in gold armour and Guinevere in gold hair, and all these knights and heroes
and beauties, and purple landscapes, and misty gray
lakes in which you have made me live.   They seem like
facts to me, since about three weeks ago (three weeks,
or a month, was it?) when I read the book.   It is on
the table yonder, and I don't like, somehow, to disturb
it,—but the delight and gratitude!   You have made me
as happy as I was as a child in the *Arabian Nights*,
every step I have walked in England has been a sort
of Paradise to me.   (The landlord gave two bottles of
his claret, and I think I drank the most), and here I
have been lying back in the chair and thinking of these
most delightful *Idylls*, my thoughts being turned to you;
what could I do but be grateful to that surprising genius
which has made me so happy?   Do you understand that
what I mean is all true, and that I should break out
were you sitting opposite with a pipe in your mouth?
Gold and purple and diamonds, I say, gentlemen, and
glory and love and honour, and if you haven't given me
all these, why should I be in such an ardour of gratitude?   But I have out of that dear book the greatest
delight that has ever come to me since I was a young
man; to write and think about it makes me almost
young, and this I suppose is what I am doing, like an
after-dinner speech."[1]

Such a letter from such a man is an event in any
life.   But what Thackeray said was scarcely stronger
than what the press and the best-known men in the
country were saying.

[1] *Life,* i. p. 444.

Here at last was the great "national poem" for which the *Edinburgh Review* had pleaded since the 1842 volume. Yet amongst the most faithful there was a certain regret. Mr. Leslie Stephen admits that after the *Idylls* he was somewhat an alien from the inner circle of the truly devout, FitzGerald was not enthusiastic, and Ruskin wrote, doubtful "about that increased quietness of style". With that insight which so often has distinguished his judgments, he puts the whole case against the *Idylls* into four lines, admirable in their courtesy:—

"As a description of various nobleness and tenderness the book is without price; but I shall always wish it had been nobleness independent of a romantic condition of externals in general".[1]

He demands from the poet "the intense masterful and unerring transcript of an actuality"; something nearer to real human life. "This seems to me", he writes, "the true task of the modern poet. And I think I have seen faces and heard voices by road and street side which claimed or conferred as much as ever the loveliest or saddest of Camelot."

But these were only the voices of a small minority; and from 1860 onwards it may be said with certainty that Tennyson commanded the widest public that a living poet has ever addressed. Men and women read him in the Australian bush as they read him in the crowded houses of New York, or among the chimneys of a Lancashire manufacturing town; they read him, and they never stinted him of praise. He had entered in on his heritage, and it was a great one.

[1] *Life*, ii. p. 453.

Chapter III.

Tennyson's Treatment of Love.

There is in the *Life* a very remarkable letter from Lord Dufferin to the poet, in which the writer expressed his gratitude for what may fairly rank among the greatest of all services.

"For the first twenty years of my life", he says, "I not only did not care for poetry, but to the despair of my friends absolutely disliked it, at least so much of it as until that time had fallen in my way. In vain my mother read to me Dryden, Pope, Byron, Young, Cowper, and all the standard classics of the day; each seemed to me as distasteful as I had from early infancy found Virgil. . . . Soon afterwards I fell in with a volume of yours, and suddenly felt such a sensation of delight as I never experienced before. A new world seemed open to me, and from that day, by a constant study of your works, I gradually worked my way to a thorough appreciation of what is good in all kinds of authors." [1]

That is, put in an extreme case, the service which each poet renders to his generation or his age. He reveals to it the beauty and colour of life, as it is interpreted by art. Byron had done the same for a generation earlier, had done it for Tennyson himself in boyhood. How far back may be traced the new ascendency is matter for conjecture, but one may say with confidence that almost every lover of literature who speaks our language, born since 1830, has begun his own personal pursuit of poetry with Tennyson's love poems. There are, of course, minds among young people who seize from the first upon those poems, with *In Memoriam* at their head, which embody Tennyson's central thought, his pe-

[1] *Life*, i. p. 427.

culiar message. But the natural taste of youth in
poetry is for love poetry. It is the awakening consciousness of the sex attraction that demands to find
itself expressed in a harmony of words; and just as
that is the first passion in the lovers of poetry, so
also it is the poet's first inspiration. That is to say,
Tennyson was the first poet that most of us cared
about when we were young, and what we cared for
especially was his love poetry. As we grew older
we probably found that there was a great deal to
be said on the subject which Tennyson had not attempted to say. We found, most of us, in Browning a stronger passion, beside which the vague
aspirations of youth after an ideal of beauty seemed
unsatisfying; and though we still admired Tennyson, we admired him now for other excellences. But
none the less, his love poetry remains historically
and logically the first thing to be considered.

If one looks at the Juvenilia one sees just one
poem, *The Supposed Confessions of a Second-rate
Sensitive Mind*, which is interesting for what it
says—only one which is a document in the poet's
spiritual biography. It is also by far the least
interesting and least accomplished in point of form
and style. Nearly all the rest are experiments in
metre, the work of a young artist trying what he
could do with language. From that point of view
they will have to be considered later on. The point
to note at present is, that they are mostly about
women—imaginary women, the ideals built up
about some pretty face or attractive personality.
You have the Madelines and Adelines, Lilians,
Margarets, Kates, and the rest, elaborately described in phrases that one remembers for their
beauty, but the women are never individualized by
a single human touch. The boy who wrote these
things had certainly been in love with the desire to
be in love, but never got beyond himself so far as

to realize what is meant by passion. In *Oriana*
he writes a ballad, telling the tragic end of a love,
and he writes it chiefly to ring the changes upon
musical syllables. In *Mariana* there is indeed a
generalized study of passion—a woman's yearning
for the absent—but practically the poem is a study
in landscape effects. Like a boy, when he sees the
beauty of nature, or its suggestion, he sees it as a
setting for some vague dream of love. The one
poem of this period, *The Lover's Tale*, which attempts definitely to portray passion, was suppressed,
and only published in self-defence years afterwards;
and a very curious poem it is. The whole is
wrapped in a haze of wild and whirling words out
of which you gather that there is a boy very much
in love. But whom is he in love with? The girl is
the shadow of a shadow, a boy's dream. He loves
her because she is a girl and he is a boy, not
because he is he and she is she. The definite and
irresistible attraction between two individual natures
has not yet dawned upon him; only the vague impulse of sex towards sex and youth towards youth.

In the volume of 1832 there were two distinct
attempts to render passion: *Fatima* and *Mariana in
the South*. In each the poet was working with pure
imagination in the effort to show the love of woman
—passion simply in its most naked form of complete abandonment. Why these women love, whom
they love, the poet never stops to tell us; they are
simply pictures of passion. Mariana dwells in
solitude—a solitude of the South, where burning
sunshine drives all life out of the open to seek for
shelter, but at the heart of this solitude is a sleepless
longing. In *Fatima* almost for the only time Tennyson paints the physical traits of passion:—

> Last night, when some one spoke his name,
> From my swift blood that went and came

A thousand little shafts of flame
Were shiver'd in my narrow frame.
　O Love, O fire! once he drew
　With one long kiss my whole soul thro'
　My lips, as sunlight drinketh dew.

Women have praised *Fatima*, and in this matter
they should be judges. But it is interesting to
note how unlike is this to Tennyson's portrayal of
love in man.   Nowhere is this self-surrender hinted
at; always the man's desire is to master—to be

　　Lord of the pulse that is lord of my breast

And it is curious to note how frequently in the love
idylls man is put into an attitude of condescension.
So it is in *The Miller's Daughter*. . The lover has
to soothe away the apprehensions of his Alice, and
love her the better for her fears; he is conscious
that she will do him credit, even when she cannot
make up her mind about the dress in which she
ought to be seen by his mother. In *The Lord of
Burleigh* the promoted bride feels herself unequal
to the splendours of her lot, and droops under her
lord's superiority.   Even the Gardener's Daughter
is very much in the attitude of the Beggar Maid
before King Cophetua.   This does not alter the
beauty of the poems—*King Cophetua* is admirable,
and *The Gardener's Daughter* a miracle of luxuriant
word-painting; but after all, one looks in vain
through all this for the authentic note of passion.
This Cupid is charming, bowered about with roses,
and attended by a procession of prospective babies,
but he is a very domestic deity, not the " lord of
terrible aspect" who lives in *Romeo and Juliet* or
Antony and Cleopatra.   And the interminable condescension of the hero grows irritating in the long
run. In *Edwin Morris* there is a kind of preliminary
sketch of *Locksley Hall*; we find the slight, pretty

little person who is terrified by her parents out of
the nobler fortunes which awaited her as the chosen
of a heroic character. In *Locksley Hall* itself, which
is a real love poem, one has to admit that the note
of passion is there. But all the same one comes
upon the old central idea. Amy has proved unworthy of the high destiny that was in store for her.
There is condescension in the wooing.

And I said, "My cousin Amy, speak, and speak the truth to me,
Trust me, cousin, all the current of my being sets to thee".

In a word, the lover will be graciously pleased to
love her. Then come the magnificent lines that
would redeem a hundred imperfections—though it
is not imperfections that one has to allege: this
fault is of the very essence.

Love took up the harp of Life, and smote on all the chords with
    might;
Smote the chord of Self, that, trembling, pass'd in music out of
    sight.

I do not believe that love ever induced this young
man to forget himself. He is always conscious of
his improving influence upon the submissive Amy
—and when she deserts him, he reproaches her
with forsaking the ideal—

Is it well to wish thee happy?—having known me—to decline
On a range of lower feelings and a narrower heart than mine?

Heaven forgive you for a prig! is the inevitable
comment. Of course the thing is human nature,
but it is not agreeable human nature. Still, it is
genuine love poetry. But in the 1832 volume there
had already appeared one poem, *The Sisters*, which
was really tense with passion. That made it apparent that, if Tennyson avoided subjects where
men and women were to be seen transfigured, and

acting either above or below their natural selves, it was not because he could not conceive a love that might be inseparable from hate, and might conflict rather than harmonize with the whole nature of the lover.   And among the poems which appeared first in 1842 was one that breathes the very spirit of the conflict between flesh and spirit, where the two are so interpenetrated with one another that their voices can hardly be distinguished.   The man who wrote these lines in *Love and Duty* certainly knew what passion was, and knew how to stamp its features:—

> Ill-fated that I am, what lot is mine
> Whose foresight preaches peace, my heart so slow
> To feel it!   For how hard it seem'd to me
> When eyes, love-languid thro' half tears, would dwell
> One earnest, earnest moment upon mine,
> Then not to dare to see! when thy low voice,
> Faltering, would break its syllables, to keep
> My own full-tuned,—hold passion in a leash,
> And not leap forth and fall about thy neck,
> And on thy bosom (deep-desired relief!)
> Rain out the heavy mist of tears, that weigh'd
> Upon my brain, my senses and my soul!

It is only just to point out that a man with this power at his command had an easy range over scenes that must always excite, and if he left them unwritten, most likely did so from a sense of the responsibility that weighs upon an artist in painting such emotions.   Yet the truth is rather that Tennyson conceived of the true subject for poetry as lying, not in passion, but in the mastery of passion.   In *Love and Duty* he lets himself go far enough to show the conflict, but the attitude is still the same.   Decision rests with the man, and it must be owned that this situation has in it something unsympathetic.   It is the converse of the relation we find in Sidney's *Astrophel and Stella*, where the strife of love and duty is so beautifully rendered, but it is the woman who resists. Tennyson seems to lack all feeling for the woman's natural reaction against what Stevenson, writing a very kindred scene in *Weir of Hermiston*, calls "the schoolmaster that is present in all men":

> Then followed counsel, comfort, and the words
> That make a man feel strong in speaking truth.

The relation is still that of the hero in *Locksley Hall* to his Amy; true enough, but, as I have said, unsympathetic. The schoolmaster is never a taking character. Yet one forgives much for the beautiful lines, where the lover consigns even the shadow of himself to oblivion:

> Should it cross thy dreams,
> O might it come like one that looks content,
> With quiet eyes *unfaithful to the truth*.

But in the next line the moralist comes back, not wholly to be forgiven even for the sake of his exquisite conclusion.

Of course one has to remember that Tennyson, in this as in most things, reflected the ideals of his age. It was the period of submissive heroines. In 1846 *Vanity Fair* appeared, and Amelia is only a constant Amy; while it really seems clear from a letter of Thackeray's, published the other day, that her creator felt for Becky Sharp little of that sympathy which few of us nowadays can deny her. Nor were the poems of which I have spoken the only love poems. *The Talking Oak*, an extraordinary *tour de force* in style, easily overstepping the line which separates *vers de société* from poetry, was not more impassioned than a compliment can be. But in *The Sleeping Beauty* there was love poetry of the most exquisite and undeniable charm. An exquisite half-comic fancy in the pictures of the sleeping court alternates with romantic imagination in the figures of the Sleeping Princess and the

> Fairy prince, with joyful eyes
> And lighter-footed than the fox ;—

and the poem closes in the lovely canto of *The Departure*, where one feels under and through the mere beauty of words all the symbolism of the story, all the quickening of the sleeping pulses that love wakens into life.

> And on her lover's arm she leant,
>   And round her waist she felt it fold,
> And far across the hills they went
>   In that new world which is the old:
> Across the hills, and far away
>   Beyond their utmost purple rim,
> And deep into the dying day
>   The happy princess follow'd him.

Unhappily, however, this gem has been put into an early Victorian setting. In the volume of 1830 appeared the stanzas which describe the Sleeping Beauty—a gorgeous example of luxuriant imagination. To these Tennyson added others completing the legend, some inferior, some even better, but all harmonizing. Only, when the thing was done he could not be content without a comment. Already he was dogged by the spirit of didactic allegory, and he moralizes the legend, whose meaning he had hinted sufficiently in the verse I quoted above. Some of the moralizing is done with admirable felicity, though all of it would be better away, but it lapses toward the end into the sheer commonplace of this address to his " Lady Flora ":—

> In the name of wife,
> And in the rights that name may give,
> Are clasped the moral of thy life,
> And that for which I care to live.

The same tendency made itself perceptible more conspicuously in his next volume. *The Princess*, considered as poetry, suffers from the vice of being too apposite. Questionings as to the true position of woman in society, the true relation between the sexes, and the true training for female minds and bodies, were in the air, and Tennyson, after his wont, thought to-day what England was going to think to-morrow. It is the Nemesis of advanced thought that the heresy of one age becomes the platitude of the next, and Tennyson was in the eyes of the orthodox always mildly heretical. Every age likes a new and appropriate moral, but the more close-fitting and appropriate the moral the more certainly will it be superseded. Poetry, if it is to last, must deal with the truths that are neither old nor new—truths that each generation in the cycles of mankind rediscovers for itself. Tennyson of course knew this well enough, and by an amazing *tour de force* he succeeded in uniting his poetical pamphleteering on the question of woman's rights to the eternal freshness of a love story. He constructed an elaborate extravaganza adorned with every possible virtuosity of style, clothing a sort of glorified school-treat in a gorgeous mantle of words, and not shrinking even from the sublime, when the sublime came closest to the ridiculous. What could be finer than Ida's pæan of triumph?

> Our enemies have fall'n, have fall'n ; the seed,
> The little seed they laughed at in the dark,
> Has risen and cleft the soil and grown a bulk
> Of spanless girth that lays on every side
> A thousand arms and rushes to the Sun.

And yet, when you think that this is sung by a lecturer on astronomy to celebrate the triumph of mail-clad knights who contend for the right of women to go to college, the reflection is saddening.

Nowhere in literature—not even in *Cyrano de Ber-
gerac*—is there so much poetical genius squandered
upon a ridiculous framework as in *The Princess*.

And yet, when one was young, probably one
liked the *Princess* better than anything else. When
one was very young, it filled the mind with noble
aspirations towards improving the intellectual condition of one's less fortunate sisters and cousins.
Then there were, and there are, always the songs,
happily detachable from the context; songs that
may rank with the very best in their kind that any
literature has to show. But lastly and chiefly, one
liked *The Princess* for the love story. It is hard to
believe that one liked the earlier passages where
the prince conducts his wooing in a petticoat; but
all the scene of his recovery—Ida's nursing of the
wounded prince, and the gradual birth of love in
her, described in lines which every one knows by
heart; the prince's awakening and his appeal to the
"sweet dream" to fulfil itself—verses exquisite in
their movement;—Ida's yielding, and the beauty of
her womanhood celebrated in a passage where the
pomp of words rings like a triumphal march—all
this breathes the very spirit of love poetry. Then,
immediately following on this, come the lyric and
the "small sweet idyll" which the princess reads
to her lover—poems which, set as they are in that
high-wrought luxuriance of style, have to be, and
are, χρύσῳ χρυσότερα—diamonds within gold.

The final passage has magnificent lines and noble
thoughts in plenty, but when the Prince awakes to
full consciousness I fear the schoolmaster revives
with him. By the necessity of the situation we are
reminded of the ridiculous story with which this
fabric of beauty is compacted, like a piece of rich
stained glass in a doll's house; by the nature of
Tennyson we are again brought face to face with
the moralizer. Man resumes his rôle as the exhor-

ter and uplifter; and the last line of the poem sums
up his whole attitude—

Lay thy sweet hands in mine and trust to me.

For a youth who began by masquerading in petti-
coats this is hopelessly incongruous; and even if
one accepts the incongruity as part of the poet's
scheme, the moral stand-point involved is, one
must repeat, more admirable than sympathetic.

But when all is said, there is no sort of doubt as
to the rank of Tennyson's best love poetry. *Maud*
puts an end to cavillings; for *Maud* is simply the
greatest love poem that has been written since
Shakespeare. It is the most original thing that
Tennyson ever did, the most complete expression,
not perhaps of the man, but of the poet in the man;
and merely from a technical point of view it was
absolutely novel. English literature presented no
example of a lyrical drama before *Maud*; and the
free use in serious poetry of common names for
common things had never before been carried so
far; the imaginary barrier between poetry and prose
was finally broken down, and no poet, after the
storm raised by academic critics against passages
in *Maud* had subsided, could possibly find himself
damned to a dialect or jargon. *Maud* is a triumph
in many ways: triumphant as an innovation in
style and form; triumphant in its proof how a
poet can throw into his crucible the most varied material,—comments upon passing events, a patriot's
anger, observation of nature more minute than
Wordsworth's,— and yet fuse them all into an
inseparable whole by the dominant unity of a central emotion. But above all it is a triumph of sustained passion. Long as it is, complex as is the
story it tells, one never thinks of anything but the
love interest. The lover's bitterness against the

world is simply the measure of his need for love.
The one drawback of the poem is of course that the
protagonist is a character little formed to attract
sympathy.   Touched with madness, he is at the
worst "splenetic, personal, base"; at the best morbid.   Still, one has to take inspiration as it comes;
and it must be remembered that Tennyson's ideal
man, the "still strong man in a blatant land", is
not one to be so shaken, even by love.   The hero
of *Maud* is not heroic.   If you come to that, Romeo
is not a particularly admirable person.   Romeo is
attractive, no doubt; and Maud's lover, this mor-
bidly self-centred person, quick to construe looks
into contempt and vehemently eager to sting back,
is repellent.   But he is in love as much as ever
Romeo was, and no one has ever rendered the
healing touch of love upon the fevers of wounded
pride with more subtlety than Tennyson in the
early cantos.   The story no doubt imposed itself
upon him; he hardly chose it; for the history of
the poem is curious.

In 1837 was published in *The Tribute*, a miscellany compiled by Lord Northampton for a charitable
purpose, that canto which in the finished poem re-
presents the lover's mind brooding on the first
tidings of Maud's death.   It is so interesting to
see this germ of a great poem that I transcribe it,
italicizing the lines which were altered or suppressed in *Maud*.

STANZAS BY ALFRED TENNYSON, ESQ.

I.

Oh that 'twere possible,
  After long grief and pain,
To find the arms of my true-love
  Round me once again!

II.

When I was wont to meet her
  In the silent woody places
    Of the land that gave me birth,
  We stood tranced in long embraces
Mixt with kisses sweeter, sweeter,
    Than any thing on earth.

III.

A shadow flits before me—
  Not thou but like to thee.
Ah, God! that it were possible
  For one short hour to see
The souls we loved, that they might tell us
  What and where they be.

IV.

It leads me forth at evening,
  It lightly winds and steals
In a cold white robe before me
  When all my spirit reels
At the shouts, the leagues of lights.
  And the roaring of the wheels.

V.

Half the night I waste in sighs,
  In a wakeful doze I sorrow
For the hand, the lips, the eyes,
  For the meeting of to-morrow,
    The delight of happy laughter,
The delight of low replies.

VI.

Do I hear *the pleasant ditty*
    That I heard her chant of old?
  But I wake—my dream is fled
Without knowledge, without pity,
    In the shuddering dawn behold
  By the curtains of my bed
    That abiding phantom cold.

VII.

Then I rise; the eave-drops fall
  And the yellow vapours choke
    The great city, sounding wide.

The day comes—a dull red ball
   Wrapt in drifts of lurid smoke
   On the misty river-tide.

VIII.

Thro' the hubbub of the market
   I steal, a wasted frame;
It crosseth here, it crosseth there—
Thro' all the crowd, confused and loud,
   The shadow still the same.
And on my heavy eyelids
   My anguish hangs like shame.

IX.

Alas for her that met me,
   That heard me softly call—
Came glimmering through the laurels
   At the quiet even-fall,
In the garden by the turrets
   Of the old *Baronial* Hall.

X.

Then the broad light glares and beats;
And the *sunk eye* flits and fleets,
   And will not let me be.
I loathe the squares and streets,
And the faces that one meets,
   Hearts with no love for me;
Always I long to creep
To some still cavern deep,
And to weep and weep and weep
   My whole soul out to thee.

XI.

Get thee hence, nor come again,
   Pass and cease to move about—
Pass, thou death-like type of pain,
   Mix not memory with doubt.
'Tis the blot upon the brain
   That *will* show itself without.

XII.

Would the happy spirit descend
   In the chamber or the street
      As she looks among the blest?

Should I fear to greet my friend,
  Or to ask her "Take me, sweet,
    To the region of thy rest"?

XIII.

But she tarries in her place
And I paint the beauteous face
  Of the maiden, that I lost,
    In my inner eyes again,
Lest my heart be overborne
By the thing I hold in scorn,
  By a dull mechanic ghost
    And a juggle of the brain.

XIV.

I can shadow forth my bride
  As I knew her fair and kind
    As I woo'd her for my wife;
She is lovely by my side
    In the silence of my life—
  'Tis a phantom of the mind.

XV.

'Tis a phantom fair and good
  I can call it to my side,
    So to guard my life from ill,
Tho' its ghastly sister glide
    And be moved around me still
With the moving of the blood
    That is moved not of the will.

XVI.

Let it pass, the dreary brow,
  Let the dismal face go by,
Will it lead me to the grave?
    Then I lose it: it will fly:
Can it overlast the nerves?
    Can it overlive the eye?
But the other, like a star,
Thro' the channel windeth far
    Till it fade and fail and die,
To its Archetype that waits
Clad in light by golden gates,
Clad in light the Spirit waits
  To embrace me in the sky.

Comparison shows that of these sixteen stanzas which describe the lover as haunted by a physical illusion, the last three are struck out in *Maud*. The first five are all but identical, save that in the fifth two exquisite lines are added. The sixth stanza in *Maud* ("'Tis a morning pure and sweet") is new; the seventh is a good deal modified from the sixth of these; lines are inserted that refer to the duel; and it is followed by the verse which here stands as eleventh. The next three (vii., viii., and ix. above) are reproduced continuously. After them comes the stanza "Would the happy spirit descend", which Tennyson seems to think makes it sufficiently clear that the "dull mechanic ghost" is not Maud's own spirit but "a juggle of the brain", and thus dispenses with the original conclusion; so in *Maud* the canto ends with the passionate cry of what is here the tenth stanza.

Years later a friend—Sir John Simeon—pointed out that the verses implied a story, and urged that it should be written; and so *Maud* came into being. Unlike the *Idylls*, *Enoch Arden*, and most of the narrative poems, it was the poet's absolute invention; it was based on no incident already recorded, and for that reason it has a peculiar interest. Madness and all kindred forms of brooding possession, the working of a mind distorted from its natural self, always had a curious fascination for Tennyson. As early as in *The Lover's Tale* one finds the notion of a person walking in visions; the prince with his "weird seizures" in *The Princess* reproduces the theme; and Lancelot's frenzy in *The Holy Grail* is yet another example. Much praise has been bestowed, and with reason, upon the scene in the madhouse which depicts the half-crazed delirium of a mind haunted by thoughts that it cannot clearly envisage. There are touches in it which Shakespeare might not disdain:

Arsenic, arsenic, sure, would do it,
Except that now we poison our babes, poor souls!
    It is all used up for that.

That is the really sudden, half-shrewd, half-childish
thrust of mad talk; and there is the pathos of a
mad complaint in this cry of the man who believes
himself dead and troubled in the grave:

O me, why have they not buried me deep enough?
Is it kind to have made me a grave so rough,
    Me that was never a quiet sleeper?

Many too have been eloquent in commendation
of the half-prophetic rhapsodies which begin and
end the poems—these denunciations of what is
sordid and criminal in modern life, those foretell-
ings of what is brighter in the prospect, which
resemble passages in the early and the later *Locksley Hall* poems.   But the real essential beauty of
Maud lies not in this fiery rhetoric, but in the love
story.   Browning has written love poems scarcely
less beautiful in a manlier key; but no one else, to
my thinking, has so well painted the sheer ecstasy
of passion.   Passion grows and spreads like a
flower out of this seed of beauty lighting on a heart
prepared for it by endless longings for something
to love; and with passion spring the inevitable
jealousies and heart-burnings; but love finds its
long-waited answer; and the strain rises from climax
to climax, through palpitating beauties, till it calms
itself for a moment in the triumph song of assurance:

I have led her home, my love, my only friend.
There is none like her, none.

This too swells into far-reaching thoughts, where
the glow of that splendour spreads itself even over
"sullen-seeming death".   And the lover, wonder-

ing at this funereal note, questions himself, and answers, in lines surely as like the lyrical mood of Shakespeare as were ever written:

> O why should Love, like men in drinking-songs,
> Spice his fair banquet with the dust of death?
>   Make answer, Maud, my bliss,
> Maud made my Maud by that long loving kiss,
> Life of my life, wilt thou not answer this?
> 'The dusky strand of Death inwoven here
> With dear Love's tie, makes Love himself more dear.'

Then come hindrances to meeting, impatience, and bitterness, checked by thoughts of love; and last of all, the wonderful rhapsody of the lover waiting in the garden, half mad with longing for the desired beauty, where his passion clothes itself in words that have the colour and the scent of every flower; where the flowers themselves grow living witnesses and answer him with intimations of *Maud's* coming, in stanzas where the gorgeous imagery heightens and cannot hide the flush of desire. It is a sin to read these verses out of their context; they are too highly wrought to stand anywhere but at the head of a mounting climax, for they breathe the very delirium of love. Elaborate and fanciful as they seem when you take them by themselves, read in their place they are nothing but the natural and inevitable utterance of passion. All Nature is on tiptoe with expectation, for we see all nature through the lover's soul. That is why the red rose may cry her coming, the white rose weep, the larkspur listen, and the lily whisper; and surely no one but Mr. Ruskin ever found a 'pathetic fallacy' in their doing so. It is the inarticulate cry of sheer passion wrought into words, as fanciful as the final stanza, yet as true to nature as its impassioned reduplication of the lyrical thought —the central motive of the song:

She is coming, my own, my sweet;
　Were it ever so airy a tread,
My heart would hear her and beat,
　Were it earth in an earthy bed;
My dust would hear her and beat
　Had I lain for a century dead;
Would start and tremble under her feet
　And blossom in purple and red.

It is a very different love poetry from this that we find in the *Idylls*—where we find it at all. *Gareth and Lynette* is the pretty fanciful tale of a youth and maiden, but not rooted in human nature. *The Marriage of Geraint* tells beautifully the sudden happiness of Enid and her worship for the great Knight who comes into her life like a burst of sunshine, rescues her, and promotes her to be his wife. The later story of her sufferings with him is the tale of patient Griselda, told with a new beauty of phrasing, but in itself, like so many of the mediæval inventions, based on a quixotic scruple of sentiment. Wifely allegiance strained to this point trenches on the ridiculous, just as do the fantastic observances by which the paladins honoured their loves. Very different is the really exquisite story of *Lancelot and Elaine*, which tells of a girl's natural passion, complete in its self-surrender, for a man who is too great to pride himself on the love he has awakened, and who, seeing it, and being bound to another, pays it all he can—his reverence and his pity. A letter of Jowett's is so striking that I cannot but quote three sentences from it:

"'The Lily Maid' seems to me the fairest, purest, sweetest love poem in the English language. It moves me like the love of Juliet in Shakspeare (though that is not altogether parallel), and I do not doubt, whatever opinions are expressed about it, that it will in a few years be above criticism.

"There are hundreds and hundreds of all ages (and

men as well as women) who, although they have not
died for love (have no intention of doing so), will find
there a sort of ideal consolation of their own troubles
and remembrances."

It is indeed the one of all the *Idylls* which seems
most likely to stand the test of time; and though,
as Jowett says, Elaine has little in common with
Juliet, this presentation of a girl's ideal passion,
with little of earthly in it but the desire to serve
and minister, may rank high among the truest love
poetry.

I cannot say as much for the other Idylls. *Pelleas
and Ettarre* seems to me simply incredible; even
the love-sick imaginings which a boy may weave
about a courtesan have reasonable limits.   The
passionate story of Tristram and Isolt has grown
cold among the moralizings of these later poems;
and Lancelot and Guinevere have been selected to
point the certainty of retribution where love is
chosen in place of duty.   What Tennyson paints
is not their passion—the central inspiration of the
whole legend for other story-tellers—but their strug-
gles with conscience, for it and against it.   It is
curious to see how cold is even his early lyric *Sir
Lancelot and Guinevere*, that tells of their ride to
Camelot "in the boyhood of the year" when the
spring was in their blood.   All that he sings of is,
not their mutual impulse to each other, but simply
her beauty:

> As fast she fled through sun and shade
> The happy winds upon her played,
> Blowing the ringlet from her braid,
> She looked so lovely as she swayed
>   Her rein with dainty finger tips,
> A man had given all other bliss,
> And all his worldly worth for this,
> To waste his whole heart in one kiss
>   Upon her perfect lips.

Yet there are just four lines in the Idyll of *Guinevere* that show what Tennyson might perhaps have done had he chosen:

> Passion pale they met
> And greeted. Hands in hands and eye to eye,
> Low on the border of her couch they sat,
> Stammering and staring. It was their last hour,
> A madness of farewells.

Still, the fact remains that he did not choose, but rather made the story a theme for magnificent moralizings, in which the king's part seems tinged with a colour of self-righteousness that would hardly have won back the erring Queen from her memory of Lancelot.   How differently the story has inspired other writers will be familiar to all who have read William Morris's *Defence of Guinevere* and his description of the lovers meeting at the tomb of Arthur.   Yet to illustrate what seems to me the natural beauty of the legend, rather than Morris's work I would quote a poem by Mr. Stephen Phillips.

THE PARTING OF LAUNCELOT AND GUINEVERE.

> Into a high-walled nunnery had fled
> Queen Guinevere, amid the shade to weep,
> And to repent 'mid solemn boughs, and love
> The cold globe of the moon; but now as she
> Meekly the scarcely-breathing garden walked,
> She saw, and stood, and swooned at Launcelot,
> Who burned in sudden steel like a blue flame
> Amid the cloister.   Then, when she revived,
> He came and looked on her: in the dark place
> So pale her beauty was, the sweetness such
> That he half-closed his eyes and deeply breathed;
> And as he gazed, there came into his mind
> That night of May, with pulsing stars, the strange
> Perfumed darkness, and delicious guilt
> In silent hour: but at the last he said:
> "Suffer me, lady, but to kiss thy lips
> Once, and to go away for evermore".

> But she replied, " Nay, I beseech thee, go!
> Sweet were those kisses in the deep of night;
> But from those kisses is this ruin come.
> Sweet was thy touch, but now I wail at it.
> And I have hope to see the face of Christ:
> Many are saints in heaven who sinned as I."
> Then said he, " Since it is thy will, I go".
> But those that stood around could scarce endure
> To see the dolor of these two: for he
> Swooned in his burning armour to her face,
> And both cried out as at the touch of spears:
> And as two trees at midnight, when the breeze
> Comes over them, now to each other bend,
> And now withdraw, so mournfully these two
> Still drooped together and still drew apart.
> Then like one dead her ladies bore away
> The heavy Queen, and Launcelot went out
> And through a forest weeping rode all night.

Among Tennyson's later work there are practically no love poems. In the three historical plays the love element is quite secondary, and thrown in as if out of obligation. Rosamund, indeed, makes love to Henry prettily enough, but the main drift of the drama is elsewhere. *The Cup* turns upon desire rather than on love, and Tennyson has not cared to do more than suggest it. As for *The Promise of May*, it is a wilderness of platitudes in the love scenes no less than elsewhere.

But there is one very remarkable poem which I think typifies that sort of revulsion from the physical aspect of passion that grew upon Tennyson with the advance of years. It is called (unhappily enough) *Happy*, and it is a dramatic lyric—the utterance of a lady whose husband has returned from the crusades a leper. She, after the strange burial service has been read by the church over "the living dead", goes to join him in his hut and accept the contagion rather than deny herself his presence. That surely is enough and to spare of tragic inspiration; but Tennyson in one of his extraordinary lapses into mechanical convention confounds the essential tragedy of the situation with a hackneyed tale of love, jealousy, and misunderstanding. The lady has to explain that if she let a stranger kiss her it was to make her husband jealous; how he went to the wars still misunderstanding, for she was too proud to explain; and how the wicked rival, coming to woo her in his absence, was struck by lightning before her eyes. All this fabrication is so much dead-weight on the poem itself—the plea of the woman to share even the misery and, as one may say, the physical damnation of the man she loves. And her plea is strange and significant.

You say your body is so foul—then here I stand apart
    Who yearn to lay my loving head upon your leprous breast.
The leper plague may scab my skin but never taint my heart;
    Your body is not foul to me, and body is foul at best.

I loved you first when young and fair, but now I love you most;
    The fairest flesh at last is filth on which the worm will feast;
This poor rib-grated dungeon of the holy human ghost,
    This house with all its hateful needs no cleaner than the beast,

This coarse diseaseful creature which in Eden was divine,
    This Satan-haunted ruin, this little city of sewers,
This wall of solid flesh that comes between your soul and mine,
    Will vanish and give place to the beauty that endures,

The beauty that endures on the Spiritual height,
    When we shall stand transfigured, like Christ on Hermon hill,
And moving each to music, soul in soul and light in light,
    Shall flash through one another in a moment as we will.

The imagination in the earlier of these verses is like the imagination of Swift, penetrating, irresistible, but essentially diseased; and the extraordinary beauty of the last stanza scarcely removes the impression. Dramatically, the verses seem to me magnificent; it is more than eloquence, it is the real fire of poetry; and the ideal of love which they present, is only the extreme form of that ideal which is present almost constantly through Tennyson's poetry—certainly from the *Idylls* onward. He saw in the spiritual side of love between the sexes—a love that if happy finds its fulfilment in marriage and children, and if unhappy sacrifices all to the ideal—the most powerful force for good in the world; and he saw in the sin of the flesh, which at its best is the choice of love before duty, the most insidious leaven of demoralization that can poison society. What he saw he preached, and though, as I think, he warped human nature somewhat in his representations of it, no man who thinks honestly can deny that his ideal is not only noble and beautiful, but true to the facts of life.

Chapter IV.

Tennyson's Views on Religion.

The chief preoccupation of Tennyson's mind throughout life was in a certain sense religious, but his intellect was essentially undogmatic. He had not the temperament of a disputant; his was a brooding mind, which arrived at its results by a slow process of which it could give no clear account. Gradually, as it gazed upon formless dark, things took shape and perspective; and the end was vision. You may search Tennyson's work from cover to cover without discovering even an attempt to give a logical account of his position. His creed sums itself up in one assertion: I see. And what he saw resolves itself into a single fact: that unless man's soul be immortal, life is meaningless and intolerable.

> Ever, ever and for ever, is the leading light of man.

His belief rests upon intuition. He *sees* that if life does not end at the grave, then at least a guess may be made at the meaning of the world; but that if the living man is finally dissolved when the worms have their will of him, all the most significant facts of existence are turned into the "tale told by an idiot". He knows perfectly well the answer to this proposition; that if a man looks hard into the dark he will certainly end by seeing, but he will see the creations of his own nerves and brain; if he strains his sense to hear, he will end by hearing, but it will be only the murmur of his own blood. The answer is unanswerable except by appeal to the truth of instinct, so far as this life is concerned. Tennyson is confident that the next life will justify him of his faith; for that is what the whole debate ends in—a question of faith. Tennyson's theology is entirely a natural theology. He bases nothing upon the historic fact of a revelation made by Christ to man; the difficulties and hopes that ally themselves with a belief in the Incarnation find little reflection in his verse; his appeal is always to the standing revelation in the heart. Few of the more definite issues are ever raised in his speculations, and none are handled with any reference to dogma. I do not think that it could be proved from his writings—not even from the opening line of *In Memoriam*—that he believed Christ to be in any literal sense the Son of God. He believed that God existed and that the soul of man was immortal; it seems a scanty equipment for one who was to be perhaps the most influential religious teacher of his century. But he also asserted for his age the right for a man to count himself a Christian on grounds other than dogmatic, and he asserted the necessity of fostering the spiritual life. That was the message for which his age cried out, and he, emphatically the prophet of his age, delivered it with an authority that grew upon him and made itself increasingly felt by those who listened. Proclaiming the lawfulness of doubt, he also proclaimed that the end of doubt, if doubt meant anxious inquiry, might be vision.

There is a kind of ingratitude, inevitable, no doubt, but still ungracious, from which those suffer who have fought the battles of progress in any direction. The accomplished fact becomes a commonplace, and a new generation rates lightly the struggle which it cost. We read *Essays and Reviews* now, laugh to find that one of these *enfants perdus* of free thought within the Church is now Archbishop of Canterbury, and wonder which of all these now admitted propositions could have raised such a disturbance in its day. But that does not alter the fact that conspicuous moral courage was needed to be among that band, and it must be remembered that Tennyson's religious speculations date from an earlier day still. When he went to college the atmosphere was tense with the death struggle, as it then seemed, between faith and science. The wave of pity for suffering humanity, which since has turned the universities into nurseries of socialist speculation, had not made itself felt; all minds were preoccupied with the question whether it were permissible to doubt, or possible not to doubt. Science was busy pointing out discrepancies between the facts it revealed and the narrative set down in the first chapters of *Genesis*, and for the moment men felt, or seemed to feel, that the whole fabric of Christianity stood or fell with the literal authenticity of the account of Creation. Tennyson, living in a group of serious-minded young men, keenly alive to the intellectual movements of their time, listened to much discussion and apparently spoke little. But the question had a special bearing for him, since he

more than any other of that circle was impregnated
with the teaching of science.   Astronomy was more
to him than a bare string of facts; it was a key
opening the door to imaginative vision.   He saw
the world whirling in limitless space among other
stars past telling; the story of the heavens spoke to
him like the revelation of a human face.   He knew
the surface of the earth minutely, and he drank
eagerly the knowledge which could tell him how
the rocks took their shape, why this was ribbed and
that twisted.   And pondering on the relation between higher and lower types, he actually thought
out for himself in some vague form Darwin's great
hypothesis.   Thus nothing could induce him to see
in science an enemy to be baffled and fought with,
but rather an ally or a guide.

No one could read his poems and not feel that
this man at least was shutting his mind against
nothing; and consequently the world, sick at heart
with hearing door after door crashed to in the face
of its most intimate hopes, welcomed his utterance,
which told them that beyond the facts which science
could explain there lay others utterly inexplicable
except upon a supposition that would leave to man
his aspirations.   In short, Tennyson propounded a
via media between dogmatic Christianity and dogmatic materialism, and the compromise was welcome.

Few as Tennyson's definite convictions would
appear to have been, he did not reach them without
pain; and among that small number of poems in
his work which one must take to be strictly autobiographical is a piece in the Juvenilia called the
*Supposed Confessions of a Second-rate Sensitive
Mind.*   It is, as I have already pointed out, by
far the least accomplished in style of these early
verses, for the very good reasons that in the others
the young poet had nothing particular to say, and
saw his subject detached from himself; here he is

embarrassed with the tangle of his own thoughts, and must think rather about the thing to be said than the way of saying it. The title, too, with its assumption of contempt, is sufficiently characteristic; it is just how a youth would seek to conceal the real intimacy of the relation between what he had uttered and the depths of his own nature. Historically, of course, the poem is not autobiographical; Tennyson's mother was alive for long years after it was written; but there can be little question but that, to a nature so strongly bound to home, the first bitterness of religious doubts would be the dread of estrangement from those whom the doubter held dearest. Doubt would certainly have seemed, to the household in which Tennyson was bred, an impious and evil thing, and far harder to relinquish than his own faith would have been his faith in the faith of others.

> Men pass me by;
> Christians with happy countenances—
> And children all seem full of Thee!
> And women smile with saint-like glances
> Like Thine own mother's when she bow'd
> Above Thee, on that happy morn
> When angels spake to men aloud,
> And Thou and peace to earth were born.

And again he cries out after the sweetness of "a common faith . . . a common scorn of death"; and after the blessed tranquillity of infancy, and the days when he prayed at his mother's knee. Why cannot he pray now when she prays, and

> Bow myself down where thou hast knelt?

Why cannot her prayers for him avail to save his faith? Is it the sin of pride that hinders? "Alas!" he answers:

> I think that pride hath now no place
> Nor sojourn in me. I am void,
> Dark, formless, utterly destroyed.

" Why not believe, then?"   And he answers with
a question.   Why does not the sea mirror heaven
with the stillness of an inland lake?   He is all
shaken in spirit,

> Moved from beneath with doubt and fear.

The first impulse of his youth had been courage.

> It is man's privilege to doubt,

for some day truth may emerge, a perfect image,
from this chaos.   Is man to be as the ox or sheep
who feeds in the meadow, neither foreknowing his
end nor aspiring beyond death?   Is it not man's
duty to grapple with doubt?

> Shall we not look into the laws
> Of life and death, and things that seem,
> And things that be, and analyse
> Our double nature, and compare
> All creeds till we have found the one,
> If one there be?

Yet to this comes no confident answer, only a cry
for guidance:

> Oh teach me yet
> Somewhat before the heavy clod
> Weighs on me, and the busy fret
> Of that sharp-headed worm begins
> In the gross blackness underneath.

And the end is half a cry, half a groan:

> O weary life! O weary death!
> O spirit and heart made desolate!
> O damned vacillating state!

I have quoted largely from this poem, because it
is, I think, little studied, and because it seems a
valuable document.   We have there, at all events,
a plain enough picture of morbid gloom, and it

was probably the influence of Hallam, with his sanguine optimism, that roused Tennyson from this black-blooded state. Tennyson's letters to his friend were all destroyed after Arthur Hallam's death by the elder Hallam, and so one is left to conjecture; but *In Memoriam* stands for a record of the service done. It is a long way from the moody vacillation of these lines to the confident hope and the conscious dignity of the *In Memoriam* stanzas. Yet Arthur Hallam's death was followed by a period of intense depression, accentuated by the disparagement in the press of the early poems. And in the curious symbolic sketch of his life which the poet wrote in one of his latest volumes— *Merlin and The Gleam*—it is probably fair to interpret the following passage not merely with a reference to the hostile criticism of Lockhart and others, but to the harassing cloud of doubts which clouded "The Gleam".

> Once at the croak of a Raven who crost it,
> A barbarous people,
> Blind to the magic,
> And deaf to the melody,
> Snarl'd at and cursed me.
> A demon vext me,
> The light retreated,
> The landskip darken'd,
> The melody deaden'd,
> The Master whisper'd
> "Follow The Gleam".

Out of the reaction against this despondency was born, so we read in the *Life*, the noble poem of *Ulysses*; and out of the despondency itself, no doubt, the longer and more definitely religious argument, *The Two Voices*. I have never been able to admire this composition, but it impressed people strongly at the time—Carlyle said it reminded him of the Book of Job—and it is very interesting historically.

The poem is an argument for and against suicide.

> Thou art so full of misery,
> Were it not better not to be?

That is the problem, and the answer is worked out
on the most general grounds.   It is a sin, says the
man, to shatter this wonderful work, this human
fabric.   And the first voice answers: Set man by
the side of a dragon-fly—(undoubtedly a disastrous
comparison for most of us so far as beauty goes).
But the man answers that Man is the crown of
Creation.   The mocking voice bids this "mould
of hopes and fears" look up through the circling
worlds of night: and then urges the pettiness of
one unit in so vast a scheme.   And so man is driven
back on his real answer—the desire to live, and he
introduces, as the strongest form of that desire, the
central motive of *Ulysses*; the passion for new
knowledge, for a horizon that widens by man's
efforts.   But here the poet is concerned to put also
the answer to this aspiration, the thought that
damps this passion.   All quest is foredoomed to
failure; the horizon must always recede, and the
span of life is so brief that all that can be achieved
in all its days is practically nothing.   Again the
man urges not a reason but an impulse, the natural
tendency to strive.   Who is to say, moreover, that
the striving and the quest will end with dissolution
of the body?   And so we strike the old Platonic
idea of re-incarnation, but now, under the influence
of modern science, thrown into a remarkable form.

> Or if thro' lower lives I came—
> Tho' all experience past became
> Consolidate in mind and frame—
>
> I might forget my weaker lot ;
> For is not our first year forgot?
> The haunts of memory echo not.

That is practically an imaginative expression of the Darwinian teaching, and in the first of these two stanzas lies to me the chief interest of the poem. The argument underlying the whole of it is not perhaps weak, but formless—a strong contrast to Browning's incisive logic—and practically, as I have already said, the only answer to the desire for death is to point out the existence of a stronger desire for life.

> Whatever crazy sorrow saith,
> No life that breathes with human breath
> Has ever truly long'd for death.
>
> 'Tis life, whereof our nerves are scant,
> Oh life, not death, for which we pant;
> More life, and fuller, that I want.

And so the poem concludes with a vision of happy people going to church on a fine morning, a passage whose connection with the rest is merely emotional, not logical. And, prompted by the "hidden hope" which this sight and the fresh breath of Nature have power to suggest, the poet does not, indeed, go to church, but wanders into the fields to commune with the joyful spirit of life which everywhere in the universe moves beside the sad spirit of death.

Another poem, kindred in thought to *The Two Voices*, and in my judgment far more interesting, is *The Vision of Sin*. Given the belief that death ends everything, there are two conclusions easily deducible for the purposes of art. If life wearies you, and has no significance beyond what the senses feel, end it. Or secondly, if life stops at the grave, *carpe diem*—make the most of it, for the profit of the senses. The former conclusion is put by the Voice that counsels suicide; the second is the philosophy preached by the worn-out sinner.

>Fill the cup, and fill the can:
>   Have a rouse before the morn:
>Every moment dies a man,
>   Every moment one is born.

It is the philosophy of Horace, but Horace puts it before us with no trace of bitterness; it is the philosophy of Omar Khayyam in whom—or in Fitz-Gerald—there is traceable a cry of revolt against the power that has flung us unconsulted into a life where the best to do is to drink. But Tennyson puts it here as the cry of despair. The sinner has drunk to the lees of pleasure—the poem opens with a magnificent passage where the whole circle of intoxication for the senses is caught up and set to a music of words—and the wine has turned to gall within him, and his speech is a devil's dance of hideous fancies. But a moral is appended. Horace and the Persian identify themselves, whether in complacency or bitterness, with their creed; Tennyson stands apart and pronounces on his sinner. His mind always shrinks from definite utterances, and he is content to put the diverse comments. Life, as it may pass from the lower to the higher, may also sink in the scale.

>Once more uprose the mystic mountain-range:
>Below were men and horses pierced with worms,
>And slowly quickening into lower forms.

There is no doubt to which slope the sinner faces; but is the downward course inevitable and irretrievable?

>At last I heard a voice upon the slope
>Cry to the summit, "Is there any hope?"
>To which an answer peal'd from that high land,
>But in a tongue no man could understand;
>And on the glimmering limit far withdrawn
>God made Himself an awful rose of dawn.

There is a fine touch of high mysteries about these lines; but there is also a fine vagueness. Yet somehow Tennyson never leaves us with the impression that he is afraid of conclusions; rather that his mind naturally tended to find repose in suspense.

Such is, I think, the opinion to be deduced from a careful reading of *In Memoriam*,—which of course, more than any other poem, embodies Tennyson's religious thought; though not perhaps in their most definite and final form, these are the conclusions of his maturity, the central teachings of his life.

The opening canto or prelude is to be taken, not as a first word, but a last commendation; it bears the date 1849, whereas some of the verses in the body of the poem were written almost directly after Hallam's death in 1834. The invocation is to Christ, "Strong Son of God", but the appeal is at once to God as Son and to God as Creator; and it sums in four lines the whole conclusion.

> Strong Son of God, immortal Love,
>   Whom we, that have not seen thy face,
>   *By faith, and faith alone, embrace,*
> *Believing where we cannot prove.*

"Thou madest man", the poem goes on; "He thinks he was not made to die, and Thou hast made him: Thou art just." The Creator is answerable for the thoughts that are part of the creature; and God is not a cheat. That is the whole thesis. Tennyson will not believe that this instinctive craving after "more life and fuller" was implanted in us by some mocking destiny; and therefore he has faith.

But in what is the faith?

> Our little systems have their day;
>   They have their day and cease to be:
>   They are but broken lights of thee,
> And thou, O Lord, art more than they.

Is Christianity one of the "little systems"?   In so far as by Christianity is meant any particular man's conception of Christianity, or even the complex of dogmas held at any moment by any church, I should say emphatically that Tennyson meant that these also were things that must change, "broken lights" to be succeeded by other broken lights.   Yet Tennyson's purpose is not to emphasize points of difference but points of kinship in religion, and the devoutest Christians would adopt the utterance of these opening stanzas.

The religious speculation in the poem only gradually develops and grows out of the first moods, in painting which Tennyson is painting his own grief. He begins indeed with a theological notion and pleads for the natural right to grieve, though death should be accounted a blessing, by one who holds

> That men may rise on stepping-stones
> Of their dead selves to higher things.

Yet sorrow prompts to despair, to the doubt of any benignant purpose in the universe.

> "The stars", he whispers, "blindly run,
> A web is woven across the sky."

To this there is for the moment no answer; the poet goes on to trace the physiognomy of grief, its common thoughts and acts—its tragic sense of other's sorrow, its pilgrimages to old haunts of happiness.   Then comes the evocation of the image of the dead, and his surroundings—the ship, and a prayer for the ship's safety—and the anxiety that this at least may be granted, a grave in English turf and a resting-place among his own.   All these early cantos deal not with thought but with feeling; they show the mind that takes its flight, like a dove, to meet the vessel, and plays round it in fancy, while the body is forgotten; then the realization of loss, the physical confirmation, like the widower's when he stretches out arms into the vacant place; and a mood answering to this, the inability to realize what has happened, so strong that if Arthur in person came and stepped out of the ship that should have borne his corpse,

> I should not feel it to be strange.

Wilder fancies too come, fear of howling winds that may be tossing and harrying the poor ghost; but all this ends with the burial, and then comes a new mood of reflection and repose. Then it is that the poet has time to take thought of the outside world, which may condemn him either because he "unpacks his heart with words", or because he wastes manhood in a useless regret while the world calls for action. And the poet answers—

> I do but sing because I must,
> And pipe but as the linnets sing:
>
> And one is glad; her note is gay,
>   For now her little ones have ranged;
>   And one is sad; her note is changed,
> Because her brood is stol'n away.

His brood is stolen; the fair companionship is broken by

> The Shadow cloak'd from head to foot,
> Who keeps the keys of all the creeds.

Death, that is, must be the only test of truth, the only possible confirmation of faith; but from this side of the veil it remains a riddle. From the beautiful stanzas which proclaim the blessedness of having loved even when one has lost, we pass to the sense of loss so closely felt at Christmas, and the hope that death is only a veil, not a severance.

There is a higher felicity in the grave than rest or
sweet sleep:

> Our voices took a higher range;
>> Once more we sang: "They do not die
>> Nor lose their mortal sympathy,
> Nor change to us, although they change".

And so the poem enters definitely on its path of
metaphysical speculation. "What is the state of
the dead?"

> When Lazarus left his charnel-cave,
>> And home to Mary's house return'd,
>> Was this demanded—if he yearn'd
> To hear her weeping by his grave?

Then for one moment, by a touch of superb poetry, a
wholly different attitude of mind is brought before
us. Mary is identified in imagination with the poet's
sister, Hallam's bride that should have been. She,
like Mary, questions nothing.

> Her eyes are homes of silent prayer.
>
>> She bows, she bathes the Saviour's feet
> With costly spikenard and with tears.

Her faith is clear in its simplicity, and to her her
lover is still living in love. Through the forms of
faith she holds to faith's essence; and it is here
that the poet speaks his warning to those who
would

>> with shadow'd hint confuse
> A life that leads melodious days.

But for himself, there must be questionings, since
to know is vital.

> My own dim life should teach me this,
>> That life shall live for evermore,
>> Else earth is darkness at the core
> And dust and ashes all that is.

And for once the answer is attempted: if Life ends, yet is it not worth while to live for the sake of love, while love can still last? Such love, the poet replies, would lose half its sweetness, "half-dead to know that it must die"; or rather, and more truly, but for the hope of a life beyond

> Love had not been,
> Or been in narrowest working shut,
>
> Mere fellowship of sluggish moods,
>   Or in his coarsest Satyr-shape
>   Had bruised the herb and crush'd the grape,
> And bask'd and batten'd in the woods.

The thirty-sixth canto, which immediately follows these lines, detaches itself from the rest. I can trace no clear connection of thought, but it is fair to supply a link. If the world be so hard to explain, what hope shall there be for man to come by the inner truth, when nature seems to point to death as the end? But, it is answered, "where truth in closest words shall fail"—where, that is, abstract reasonings have no effect—"truth embodied in a tale" is to be understanded of all. God in his wisdom dealt with mortal powers according to the measure of mortal comprehension.

> And so the Word had breath, and wrought
>   With human hands the creed of creeds
>   In loveliness of perfect deeds,
> More strong than all poetic thought.

The story of Christ's life was "truth embodied in a tale". But whether this passage implies an adhesion to the orthodox doctrines of Christianity, I cannot say, and I doubt if Tennyson either could or would have decided. But it is clear that in this canto he felt himself to be overstepping his allotted province, for the next is an apology couched in the conventional form of a rebuke from Urania,

the Heavenly Muse.   To her the Muse of Earthly
Song makes answer that she had indeed been betrayed into error, but only in loving memory.

> But brooding on the dear one dead,
>   And all he said of things divine,
>   (And dear to me as sacred wine
> To dying lips is all he said),
>
> I murmur'd, as I came along,
>   Of comfort clasp'd in truth reveal'd;
>   And loiter'd in the master's field,
> And darken'd sanctities with song.

That is, we may incidentally remark, a strong confession of the spiritual directorship exercised by
Hallam on his friend; and the thirty-sixth and
thirty-seventh cantos may fairly be construed thus:
that up to the thirty-sixth the poet had been setting
down his own speculations about death and life; in
it he repeated the truths of revealed religion, as
endeared to him by the friend who had accepted
them and spoken to him of them.

But the poem soon drifts back into its central
theme of a life naturally anticipated after death.
May not death, the poet meditates, be like marriage,
a passing from the old life to the new, a link in
the generations?   Yet it is a chilly comfort that
such hopes can afford; and there is more reality in
the vague apprehension that, even granted a continuance of both lives, they may be lost to each
other in the procession of the ages, and the later
to depart "evermore a life behind".   But against
this fear there is a recoil of feeling.   His friend
was always in advance of him, yet never so far
as not to stretch out a helping hand.   Besides,
if anything lasts, love must; and by a beautiful
adaptation of the Platonic theory, the poet conceives of our souls as flowers that take their colour
and charactery from "silent traces of the past".

Thus when in the "spiritual prime" the soul re-
awakens, love must waken with it too.   Whether
in death there be consciousness he will not decide,
or whether it be merely sleep.   But—if I follow
rightly the very complex stanzas in the forty-fourth
and forty-fifth cantos—in the grown man there is
oblivion of the past; yet now and then comes some
unaccounted memory, "a little flash, a mystic hint".
So too among the happy dead, there may be a
sudden memory of the earlier life in which the
happy spirit may recall the one he loved.   Yet this
does not suffice to allay the poet's desire for com-
munion; and the argument leads to a hope of less
fleeting glimpses.   It is only the baby who has
not the sense of separate existence, "has never
thought that 'this is I'".   But the senses teach
him—

> As thro' the frame that binds him in
> His isolation grows defined.

The lesson thus taught him by the "separateness
of blood and breath" is never forgotten; else to
what end were they given,

> Had man to learn himself anew
> Beyond the second birth of Death?

And though in this life the path behind us, which
we have travelled in our progress of development,
is dark, "shadowed by the growing hour", yet "in
that deep dawn behind the tomb" there can be no
blackness.   The landscape of the past will lie clear
from margin to margin, and love, not circumscribed
to those few years of earthly knowledge, will shed
over it "a rosy warmth from marge to marge".   For
against the thought that after death each separate
self may fuse into the "general soul" the poet protests; such a belief

Is faith as vague as all unsweet:
　　Eternal form shall still divide
　　The eternal soul from all beside;
And I shall know him when we meet.

But to this belief, it will be seen, the seeker is led
by no other guide than hope.　He interprets rightly
the aspiration of the lover, which is no vague longing but definite desire to meet again the loved one;
and the reason for believing that this aspiration
will be gratified is just the same as for believing in
an after life.　The aspiration is natural to man, and
God made him with it, therefore the aspiration will
be answered.

Yet the poet knows well that his "brief lays of
sorrow born" cannot be held to close "grave
doubts and answers here proposed".　He admits
that Sorrow takes doubts "and makes them vassals
unto Love", to find some solace; and it is little
solace: for we go back to the cry of anguish, the
petition for presence of the dead.　But then, with
the thought of the dead always at hand, comes
another wave in the tide of speculation (for the
movement of the poem is rather that of wave after
wave than step after step in an ascent; the march
is bounded by the point whence it set out).　Do we
indeed desire the dead beside us—that they may
see into our hearts?　Whose heart will bear the
scrutiny?　Yet the dead watch, like God, with
large allowance for human frailty.　Can we therefore, who live, make the like allowance?　Can we
preach that human frailty matters little in the long
account? and if so, may not divine Philosophy become "procuress to the lords of hell"?

Once again the poet falls back on his cry of hope
and faith, "that somehow good will be the final
goal of ill"; but the world offers little confirmation.
Nature squanders the single life to save the type:
is God more careful than Nature, or at strife with

her? Even the type passes: may not man, too, pass? even man

> Who trusted God was love indeed,
>   And love Creation's final law—
>   Tho' Nature, red in tooth and claw
> With ravine, shriek'd against his creed.

And once again there is no answer but in hope. It is in passages like these, where Tennyson admits unquestioningly to the fullest the hard records discovered by science in the rocks and stones, while he doubts and questions of the truth which the Bible and all the framework of Christianity affirm, that he seemed to the mind of his own day to border upon heresy. To us such writings seem scarcely to bear upon religion. We assume that the facts of geology are facts, which reason cannot ignore. The facts of revelation reason must put into a wholly different category; and here was his service to the religious thought of his time, that he led the way in accepting what must be accepted, and in directing the battle where the battle can be fought. He served at once free-thought and religion in a way that no divine, who is in a sense a soldier set to defend certain positions irrespective of his personal convictions, could ever have done.

After this fifty-sixth canto, which states the case for despair at its strongest, there is a slackening in the tension of thought. One might almost say that a series closes with the fifty-seventh canto and a new one opens with the fifty-eighth. The poem turns from the problems of the universe, as they are evoked by the stimulus of sorrow, to a reflection of the passing moods of grief. Thus you have the plea of the one left on earth not to be forgotten, though his friend in that high sphere of "ransomed reason" may converse with the flower of all the ages. Out of all the question-

ing and all the imagining there has come this
certitude, arrived at by no logical process, but by
brooding meditation, that somewhere and somehow
that friend survives as that friend's self, though
emancipated from the bondage and limitations of
sense.   And so we pass to earthlier thoughts, fore-
casts of what the dead man might have attained to
on this earth; his likeness comes out to those of his
spiritual kin; the stamp of greatness is recognized
in death; and gradually the passion quiets down
till at the second Christmas all that is left of revolt
is a revolt against grief's inevitable decay.

> O grief, can grief be changed to less!

But the answer is now sane and peaceable.   The
passing of grief's poignancy means only its diffu-
sion through the whole nature, and there remains
only the abiding resentment against Death, in that

> He put our lives so far apart
> We cannot hear each other speak.

But that both lives last and will be again united is
now held for certain.   Yet still there is the "backward fancy" which pictures what might have been;
children of their mixed blood, who should have
"babbled 'Uncle' on my knee"; of lives lived together and together ended.

> And he that died in Holy Land
> Would reach us out the shining hand,
> And take us as a single soul.

There again is what seems an explicit adherence
to the truth of revealed Christianity; but a student
of Tennyson's thought must insist upon the fact
that such belief is nowhere treated as vital; it is
indeed put in this passage as the culmination of a
train of fancy and not as the pillar of a faith.

With the eighty-fifth canto new influences come

into the work. The lines are addressed to a friend who shared with him the "common grief" of Hallam's death; and they have for their message that the poet does not shut himself up in his sorrow, but rather courts human fellowship and sympathy, though what he has to offer is not the prime of love, but rather its aftermath:

> The primrose of the later year,
> As not unlike to that of Spring.

And with the renewed fellowship comes new life— "after showers, ambrosial air" to blow the fever from his cheek, and to quicken fancy with new and glowing images. Nor is this the only new sympathy. The ninety-sixth canto is plainly addressed to a woman:

> Sweet-hearted, you, whose light-blue eyes
> Are tender over drowning flies;

and to this new love the man has to justify himself —to this woman who holds that "doubt is devil-born". And the answer is, to plead the case of Hallam, one who, "perplexed in faith, but pure in deeds", did at the last "beat his music out". The lines upon the faith that lives in honest doubt have been hackneyed by endless quotation, and have for the moment lost their thrill; yet they were a message of comfort for Tennyson's generation,—for the race whose mind is reflected in Kingsley's *Yeast* and the like. The fight has been fought, and so much of peace and agreement has followed that we scarcely think of Tennyson as among the fighters; yet his tranquil wisdom perhaps won more battles than were gained by angrier disputants.

From this point onward in the poem the concentration of thought lessens; or say rather, the eye focuses itself to a wider prospect. Through all the moods of memory one can follow the widening of

the circles from the central commotion.   In a sense
the earlier moods are reviewed in calmer judgment,
and what is stated at first as the passionate clinging
to a hope becomes now settled conviction.   Science,
with the new knowledge, is not repudiated, but she
is bidden to know her place.   "She is the second,
not the first."   The truth that lives in Science is
that of a continual progress from the beast up to
man, and from man to something beyond; the lesson
is to

> Move upward, working out the beast,
> And let the ape and tiger die.

Then for a last time is stated in all its vagueness
and in all its confidence belief and the ground for
belief.

> That which we dare invoke to bless;
>   Our dearest faith; our ghastliest doubt;
>   He, They, One, All; within, without;
> The Power in darkness whom we guess;
>
> I found Him not in world or sun,
>   Or eagle's wing, or insect's eye;
>   Nor thro' the questions men may try,
> The petty cobwebs we have spun:
>
> If e'er when faith had fall'n asleep,
>   I heard a voice "believe no more",
>   And heard an ever-breaking shore
> That tumbled in the Godless deep;
>
> A warmth within the breast would melt
>   The freezing reason's colder part,
>   And like a man in wrath the heart
> Stood up and answer'd "I have felt".
>
> No, like a child in doubt and fear:
>   But that blind clamour made me wise;
>   Then was I as a child that cries,
> But, crying, knows his father near;
>
> And what I am beheld again
>   What is, and no man understands;
>   And out of darkness came the hands
> That reach thro' nature, moulding men.

And in the later cantos thought seeks once more
its centre—the friend, whose death has set afoot all
this questioning of death and life, body and soul.
That friend is seen now in air, sun and water, in
star and flower, diffused yet separate, loved and
capable of love.

> My love involves the love before;
>   My love is vaster passion now;
>   Tho' mix'd with God and Nature thou,
> I seem to love thee more and more.
>
> Far off thou art, but ever nigh;
>   I have thee still, and I rejoice;
>   I prosper, circled with thy voice;
> I shall not lose thee tho' I die.

That is the personal issue, a type for the race of its
destiny—by which man who has come "from out
the vast" and "struck his being into bounds",
having his own individuality in the separate use of
blood and breath, must progress towards those
beings that "eye to eye shall look on knowledge",
and shall live, as Hallam lives, in God—

> That God, which ever lives and loves,
>   One God, one law, one element,
>   And one far-off divine event,
> To which the whole creation moves.

Thus, by analysis of the teaching of *In Memoriam*,
we find, first a formal adherence to the creed of
Christianity expressed vaguely in the prelude and
twice over more definitely, though only incidentally,
in the body of the poem.   But we find also a con-
nected body of thought separate from this, and infinitely more vital, which interrogates nature, and
sees in nature every indication that death is the end
of a life unregarded by any higher power, where
not merely individuals are flung away, but types
and races trampled into dust; yet which also finds
in man a cry of the heart, an instinct, prompting to

believe, against the law which nature seems daily
to enforce, that there must come a survival. That
instinct Tennyson traces not to fear of death but to
love. · The breath of such life as separates itself
from concerns of the body is love, and nothing that
science can show in nature can tell how this instinct
came to be implanted. And so we are not driven
by logic to postulate a God; rather this love is in
us a perpetual revelation. That is the fabric of the
thought; upon that the whole rests. Science and
philosophy are pressed for suggestions as to what a
life after death may mean; will it be independent of
this, will it remember the deeds done in the flesh?
And the hope—it is really no more than a hope—to
which Tennyson leans so strongly that it becomes
an article of faith, is that the separate self will survive and will retain a memory of this life; for this
human life is not, as Plato made it, merely one in
a cycle of lives, but the critical and necessary step
from which we must proceed to a state of full knowledge exempt from earthly limitations, where the
souls will blossom like flowers in a garden, each
coloured and marked by its earthly past.

The more one thinks of this conception, the more
apparent is its vagueness and want of outline.
That, I think, did not trouble the poet. He was
content to convince himself that we were put here
with a purpose, and that we had a life to live
beyond the grave; for the scope and range of this
threescore years and ten pinned down to a point in
limitless space seemed to him in itself a mockery of
insignificance.

If you ask him for a more definite answer as to
what God is, he may answer you with his poem of
The Higher Pantheism—God to a man is all that is
not the man himself.

Dark is the world to thee: thyself art the reason why;
For is He not all but that which has power to feel "I am I"?

Man can never get outside himself; God has
granted to him separate existence, and with the
grant comes blindness, for by his nature he can
only see things refracted through the medium of
his own nature.

For all we have power to see is a straight staff bent in a pool.

But all about man is God if he could only see and
hear it; his whole life is a vision of God seen
through the medium of himself.   There are only
two things in the world; God and man's soul.
That is a philosophy perhaps luminous rather than
lucid; but it is just as lucid and conclusive as any
other philosophy that takes into account all the
factors in existence.   Every man to every other
man is a part of God; but there are men in whom
the vision becomes clearer, and of these, Tennyson
would say no doubt, was Hallam.   The power to
see God in others is the gift of the poet; the power
to make God seen in ourselves the gift of the saint.
No man's vision embraces the universe; no man, if
one likes to put it so, hath seen God at any time;
but the more a man sees, the more beautiful is the
vision, and Tennyson was of those who have power
to communicate what they see, or by telling us of it
to waken corresponding images in our mind.   And
his value to the world lay in this chiefly, that he
asserted that vision was vision and not a trick of
the senses.

As to Tennyson's formal religion, one can at
least assert of it the negative quality of Protestantism.   He believed profoundly in God; he dis-
believed profoundly in Rome.   In his early work,
St. Simeon Stylites, he shows, by what Browning
would call a dramatic monologue, the self-deception
of asceticism; shows it of course with a sense of its
pathos and of human pity for the follies of men.
The very uninteresting poem on Sir John Oldcastle,

the Lollard, puts the anti-papal case strongly and tersely, especially in the doctrine of transubstantiation. Tennyson was a mystic, but one so deeply imbued with the teaching of science could scarcely accept miracles, in the sense of a violation of the laws of nature; he certainly had no tolerance for the conception of a physical miracle wrought weekly or daily by every priest. But it is in the plays that his Protestantism makes itself most strongly felt. In *Queen Mary*, the most effective scene, and the only one where our whole sympathy falls to the chief actor, is that of Cranmer's final impeachment of Rome. Protestantism and the national spirit go hand in hand. Mary wishes to make her kingdom a fief of Spain and the appanage of Rome. In *Harold* the same holds. Harold is a Protestant before his time, and stands for England against the alien. Rome lends her sanction to the trick by which William seeks to bind him to irretrievable submission; Harold refuses belief in any sanctity that can be added to an oath by bones or relics. Edward, the ascetic saint, in his zeal for the church brings in the aliens to rule the church, and betrays the interests of his country. And in *Becket*, as I have elsewhere pointed out, though our sympathies go with the archbishop, Henry has the better of him in the argument. Tennyson is plainly for king against church, for civil law as against ecclesiastical domination.

In the *Idylls*, the ascetic side of chivalry is ignored or rather twisted into conformity with modern ideals. But this point must be more fully considered in relation to the whole subject of the Arthurian legend. It is sufficient here to remark that chivalry grew directly out of monasticism, and from the whole theory of monasticism Tennyson's essentially British and Protestant mind violently dissented.

On this whole matter of religious dogma one perceives an inherited bias in the poet, rather than a conviction arrived at by independent thought. It is a part of his admirable insularity. But the vital part of his teaching—for he was confessedly a teacher—relates simply to his belief in the soul's immortality. Teacher he was, but rarely a preacher. Once in the poem *Despair* he endeavoured to set out the deplorable results of a loss of faith. A man and his wife brought up in a narrow Calvinism lose faith in God, and being in poverty and disgrace, determine to end their lives together. The man is rescued, and he explains their action. The poem cannot be said to carry conviction, though it contains one great line, the despairing man's vision of the universe as—

> A fiery scroll written over with lamentation and woe.

But it is meant to put from another point of view the aspiration upon which Tennyson so strenuously insists—the desire for prolonged life lest we should be separated from those we love. Here the bitterness of death is in the parting without hope.

> Dear Love, for ever and ever, for ever and ever farewell.

That is the word on their lips as they kiss the last kiss.

> Never a cry so desolate, not since the world began,
> Never a kiss so sad, no, not since the coming of man!

It is love, not life, that despairs when faith in God and the hope of a future are taken from the world. The instinct upon which Tennyson relies is not the desire for survival, the repugnance to death. It is simply love. Man sees death in the body; and he recognizes the end, yet he hopes.

> Who forged that other influence,
> That heat of inward evidence,
> By which he doubts against the sense?

the poet asks in *The Two Voices*. And the answer comes plainer and plainer with advancing years. It is that clinging of one soul to another which we call love, and which Christianity calls the word of God. Nowhere is it put more strongly and with more eloquence than in the splendid chant called *Vastness*, which appeared after his eightieth year; written, as it would seem, after the death of his son. It is like a Greek chorus, this chant of the old prophet, as he scans the universe and sees its eternal contrasts—freedom and tyranny, wealth and destitution, faith and doubt, fame and slander—worlds sweeping past in space to their dissolution unregarded of us, the single face vanished and unremittingly mourned,—" What is it all ", he cries—

What is it all, if we all of us end but in being our own corpse-
    coffins at last,
Swallow'd in Vastness, lost in Silence, drown'd in the deeps of
    a meaningless Past?

What but a murmur of gnats in the gloom, or a moment's anger
    of bees in their hive?—

.   .   .   .

Peace, let it be! for I loved him, and love him for ever: the
    dead are not dead but alive.

That is practically the whole of his philosophy: it is a cry of the heart in revolt against knowledge. Not even the sense of this multitudinous universe can rob man of the conviction of his eternal and eternally important destiny. But it is not an eternity of stationary being that Tennyson conceives. Among the very latest of his poems are some epigrams headed " By an Evolutionist ". Here is the first stanza of them:

The Lord let the house of a brute to the soul of a man,
    And the man said, "Am I your debtor?"
And the Lord: "Not yet; but make it as clean as you can,
    And then I will let you a better".

That is Tennyson's answer to the verse in Omar Khayyam.

> Oh Thou who man of baser earth didst make,
> And even with Paradise devise the snake,
>   For all the wrong wherewith the face of man
> Is blackened, man's forgiveness give—and take.

Continued life will do for the soul what old age does already, when the man has "climbed to the snows of age",—so writes Tennyson in words that recall the answer of old Sophocles to the boy that asked him if he were past desire: "Peace, friend, I am escaped from a harsh and cruel master". He is on the snow peaks and can see all the field of the past.

> But I hear no yelp of the beast, and the Man is quiet at last,
> As he stands on the heights of his life with a glimpse of a height
>   that is higher.

That may be taken for the poet's final utterance, the last word of his wisdom upon the thought which had most occupied his life.

But two poems deserve special study by an inquirer into his philosophy. The first is *Akbar's Dream*, where he hints at a belief, or at least a sympathy with the belief, that all creeds that worship God are one and have a common origin, though in this region also there is evolution and the lower must give way to the higher; and the second, still more important, though by no means so lucid, is *The Ancient Sage*. Here you have once more the 'two voices'; that of the Sage and that of his follower, the Poet, who sings the refrain of Omar Khayyam. Death is the end, says the singer, and the true symbol to set upon your grave is the inverted wine-cup. Then for God's sake let us drink the wine, not spill it from trembling hands, nor wait till the cup be shattered. That is the philosophy to which the Sage makes answer.   Man, says the Poet, is "fancy's fool" when he believes in the Nameless.   Yet, answers the Sage,

> If thou would'st hear the Nameless, and wilt dive
> Into the Temple-cave of thine own self,
> There, brooding by the central altar, thou
> May'st haply learn the Nameless hath a voice,
> By which thou wilt abide, if thou be wise
> As if thou knewest, though thou canst not know.

What is this but Kant's Categorical Imperative, the ultimate basis of all morality?   And when the Poet chants again—

> And since—from when this earth began—
>   The Nameless never came
> Among us, never spake with man
>   And never named the Name—

the Sage strikes in with the final utterance of human reason directed upon itself, testing itself by its own tribunal:

> Thou canst not prove the Nameless, O my son,
> Nor canst thou prove the world thou movest in,
> Thou canst not prove that thou art body alone,
> Nor canst thou prove that thou art spirit alone,
> Nor canst thou prove that thou art both in one:
> Thou canst not prove thou art immortal, no
> Nor yet that thou art mortal—nay, my son,
> Thou canst not prove that I, who speak with thee,
> Am not thyself in converse with thyself,
> For nothing worthy proving can be proven,
> Nor yet disproven.

For the benefit of those not familiar with his philosophy it may be worth while to set down Kant's fundamental antinomies.   There are the self-contradictory "cosmological ideas"—conclusions as to time and space, the world, cause and freedom, the existence of God—at which the pure reason, working from such data as are available, in accordance with strict logic, must inevitably arrive:

I. *Thesis.*—The world has a beginning in time, and is limited also in regard to space.
Antithesis.—The world has no beginning and no limits in space, but is infinite in respect both to time and space.

II. *Thesis.*—Every compound substance in the world consists of simple parts, and nothing exists anywhere but the simple or what is composed of it.
Antithesis.—No compound thing in the world consists of simple parts, and there exists nowhere in the world anything simple.

III. *Thesis.*—Causality, according to the laws of nature, is not the only causality from which all the phenomena of the world can be deduced. In order to account for these phenomena, it is necessary also to admit another causality, that of freedom.
Antithesis.—There is no freedom, but everything in the world takes place entirely according to the laws of nature.

IV. *Thesis.*—There exists an absolutely necessary Being belonging to the world, either as a part or as the cause of it.
Antithesis.—There nowhere exists an absolutely necessary Being, either within or without the world, as the cause of it.

I only set this down to show that Tennyson's view is in conformity with the best modern thought; and it must be said that Kant's conclusion of the eternal self-contradiction inherent in human reason is less baffling if one sees it as a proof of life's transitoriness; if we view the world as "this half deed"—as a thing still in the making, where we can only guess at hints of the design.

Yet the sceptic singer still insists upon earth's lesson. Man grows from babyhood to maturity, from maturity to decline; what hope is there in this of progress towards a higher state?   And the Sage answers:

> The shell must break before the bird can fly.

Our body, that is, seems to him only the cage; the separable self is something bound up not *with* the body but *in* the body.   It comes, as Tennyson cries in his verses to his new-born son,

> Out of the deep, my child, out of the deep,

and it goes to the deep.   One loses in *The Ancient Sage* that keen insistence of the earlier poems on a separate consciousness continued after death.   Each self is only one "slight ripple on the boundless deep".

> But that one ripple on the boundless deep
> Feels that the deep is boundless, and itself
> For ever changing form, but evermore
> One with the boundless motion of the deep.

That is perhaps the last word of all philosophies that recognize a spirit in man distinct from the material substance.   And the last word of the Sage is that of mystical ethics: Live not for yourself but for others; curb act and thought; and one day, perhaps, rising above the finite reason, you may "Strike on the Mount of Vision".

The conclusion, as I say, is substantially that which has been reached by many minds in many ages, following many paths, all perhaps guided by the will-o'-the-wisp of a common desire.   But it is the conclusion which has been reached by the severest thinkers as well as the most visionary. Tennyson gave it a peculiar colour by importing the idea of evolution as a scientific argument.   The correlative doctrine of degeneration he never insisted upon in things spiritual, though it coloured his political thought. But the expression of his own faith, rather than his reasoned convictions, will be found unmistakable in the verses he dictated on his death-bed, his appeal to the "Silent Voices" for a leading "on and always on"; and it stands supremely beautiful in the lines, *Crossing the Bar*, which have been hackneyed in quotation but often misunderstood. Yet their meaning is plain enough. Man in this life has been a sailor in port, getting and spending; the call comes and he must put out to sea; there may be trouble as he crosses the bar that divides him from the great Beyond, or there may be a full tide to bear him over it scarce knowing. But, whether rough or smooth the going, he goes to other seas and other skies, not without guidance; and beyond the bar the guide may reveal himself and the purpose of the going.

We walk by faith; that is the conclusion of the whole matter in Tennyson's eyes; and no man who reads him fairly will deny that he recognized at once the rights of reason and its limitations. You cannot look to him for the tragic force that is in FitzGerald's stanzas; the one man sees intensely what lies under his hand, the tragi-comedy of man's lot in the earth; Tennyson, seeing through and beyond it, loses its terrible distinctness. His philosophy is not tragic, it does not stir us; but, as Maeterlinck says, where there is wisdom, tragedy can scarcely come. If your mind has the singular balance of Tennyson's, and you pin your faith to a hope, seeing clearly that it is a hope, and seeing also all the evidence that makes against it, you cannot proclaim your creed with any triumphant assurance, unless indeed you have the militant optimism of Browning. But if you see all pointing to the inevitable end, and hold to the symbol of the inverted wine-cup, as did FitzGerald or at least his original, that very hope and desire latent in you, upon which

Tennyson bases his faith, will give to your conclusion a poignant note of despair which must be always among the most moving things in literature. That is why many incline to rate FitzGerald high and depreciate Tennyson. Compromise is never very picturesque, and Tennyson, British in this as well as in everything else, held in religion to what was essentially a compromise.

Chapter V.

Tennyson's Political Opinions.

The first article in Tennyson's political creed was undoubtedly that it is a great matter to be an Englishman. This extreme sense of the national virtues has, perhaps, its drawbacks; but there is no question of the strength and genuineness of the poet's patriotism. Some of the best and most characteristic things that he ever wrote expressed once and for all the political faith of an intelligent Briton; and he was always ready to be stirred into enthusiasm by any national achievement, or any movement for national defence. This enthusiasm inspired one magnificent poem, the Ballad of *The Revenge*, and one of the most successful battle pieces ever written, *The Charge of the Light Brigade*; it also strangely betrayed him again and again into utterances where it is hard to trace the artist. The 1830 volume contained two patriotic lyrics, both of which were suppressed in later issues of the poems. The first began:

> Who fears to die, who fears to die?
> Is there any here who fears to die?

and had a chorus:

> Shout for England!
> Ho for England!

expressing altogether a patriotism more noisy than
dignified.   The other, half a century later, re-ap-
peared as the Forester's Song in the Robin Hood
play:

> There is no land like England
>   Where'er the light of day be;
> There are no hearts like English hearts,
>   Such hearts of oak as they be.
> There is no land like England
>   Where'er the light of day be;
> There are no men like Englishmen,
>   So tall and bold as they be.

And so on, *da capo*, for the women.

The triumphant sonnet upon Buonaparte was also
an early work; another upon Poland expressed
that youthful fervour on behalf of liberty, which,
as we have seen, actually tempted Tennyson and
Hallam to take part in the Spanish insurrection
against a despot.   This sympathy never wholly
deserted the poet, and the most honoured guest
who ever came to Farringford was perhaps Garibaldi.   But Tennyson's political zeal was never
like Shelley's, Byron's, or Browning's—cosmopolitan; he was British to the point of insularity.   Yet
certainly one cannot fairly object any want of
comprehensiveness to a mind which, concentrating
itself slowly on one set of phenomena, by some
slow process arrived at the very heart of the matter.
Tennyson never understood France, and his phrase
about the " blind hysterics of the Celt " is one of
those half-truths which he has denounced in a
famous verse; but he understood his own country,
and no account of the English political spirit was

ever given so luminous as that which he has condensed into a few lines:

> You ask me, why, tho' ill at ease,
>   Within this region I subsist,
>   Whose spirits falter in the mist,
> And languish for the purple seas.
>
> It is the land that freemen till,
>   That sober-suited Freedom chose,
>   The land, where girt with friends or foes
> A man may speak the thing he will;
>
> A land of settled government,
>   A land of just and old renown,
>   Where Freedom slowly broadens down
> From precedent to precedent:
>
> Where faction seldom gathers head,
>   But by degrees to fullness wrought,
>   The strength of some diffusive thought
> Hath time and space to work and spread.

This attitude towards his country lasted him through
life, and it finds a more amiable expression here
than in that passage of *The Princess* which contrasts Britain and France:

> God bless the narrow sea, which keeps her off,
> And keeps our Britain, whole within herself,
> A nation yet, the rulers and the ruled—
> Some sense of duty, something of a faith,
> Some reverence for the laws ourselves have made,
> Some patient force to change them when we will,
> Some civic manhood firm against the crowd—
> But yonder, whiff! there comes a sudden heat,
> The gravest citizen seems to lose his head,
> The king is scared, the soldier will not fight,
> The little boys begin to shoot and stab,
> A kingdom topples over with a shriek
> Like an old woman, and down rolls the world
> In mock heroics stranger than our own;
> Revolts, republics, revolutions, most
> No graver than a schoolboys' barring out;
> Too comic for the solemn things they are,
> Too solemn for the comic touches in them,

Like our wild Princess with as wise a dream
As some of theirs—God bless the narrow seas!
I wish they were a whole Atlantic broad.

But Tennyson's patriotism did not limit itself to
admiration of things as they were.   Seeing his
country's greatness, he was jealous for it, and he
preached a wise imperialism in days before the
nation at large had realized the conditions under
which it held its ascendency.   Britain was to him
the home of freedom, set by God's special mercy
within barriers of "the inviolate sea", and in his
noble *Ode on the Death of the Duke of Wellington*,
he, for the first time, urged upon his country, not
only her mission in the world, but the imperative
need to make the protecting barrier a true protection.

O Statesmen, guard us, guard the eye, the soul
Of Europe, keep our noble England whole,
And save the one true seed of freedom sown
Betwixt a people and their ancient throne,
That sober freedom out of which there springs
Our loyal passion for our temperate kings;
For, saving that, ye help to save mankind
Till public wrong be crumbled into dust,
And drill the raw world for the march of mind,
Till crowds at length be sane and crowns be just.
But wink no more in slothful overtrust.
Remember him who led your hosts;
He bad you guard the sacred coasts.
Your cannons moulder on the seaward wall!

That is a passage which to-day would be cheered
to the echo, but the poem in which it comes was
perhaps worse received than anything the poet ever
wrote.   Those were the days of the Manchester
school, and of "peace at any price".   No man
could be more eloquent in praise of commerce, that
link between the peoples, than was Tennyson a
decade later in his *Ode sung at the Opening of the
International Exhibition*:

O ye, the wise who think, the wise who reign,
From growing commerce loose her latest chain,
And let the fair white-wing'd peacemaker fly
To happy havens under all the sky,
And mix the seasons and the golden hours;
Till each man find his own in all men's good,
And all men work in noble brotherhood,
Breaking their mailed fleets and armed towers,
And ruling by obeying Nature's powers,
And gathering all the fruits of earth and crown'd with
    all her flowers.

That is the ideal set forth already twenty years
earlier in *Locksley Hall*—

The Parliament of man, the Federation of the world.

But though such Utopias had a rich incarnation in
the poet's vision, they did not blind him to the hard
realities of the present; and in his lines headed
The Third of February, 1852, he spoke his mind in
angry denunciation of the resolution of the House
of Lords:

My Lords, we heard you speak: you told us all
    That England's honest censure went too far;
That our free press should cease to brawl,
    Not sting the fiery Frenchman into war.
It was our ancient privilege, my Lords,
To fling whate'er we felt, not fearing, into words.
.   .   .   .
We feel, at least, that silence here were sin,
    Not ours the fault, if we have feeble hosts—
If easy patrons of their kin
    Have left the last free race with naked coasts!
They knew the precious things they had to guard:
For us, we will not spare the tyrant one hard word.

Tho' niggard throats of Manchester may bawl,
    What England was, shall her true sons forget?
We are not cotton-spinners all,
    But some love England and her honour yet.
And these in our Thermopylæ shall stand,
And hold against the world this honour of the land.

That was an utterance of no doubtful import. The Crimean War came two years later, but before it came the opening canto of *Maud* was written, with its outburst against the canker of peace, and its cry for the keen and bitter tonic of war; and in the mid excitement of the struggle was composed the end, which is a sort of pæan to the God of Battles:

> No more shall commerce be all in all, and Peace
> Pipe on her pastoral hillock a languid note,
> And watch her harvest ripen, her herd increase,
> Nor the cannon-bullet rust on a slothful shore,
> And the cobweb woven across the cannon's throat
> Shall shake its threaded tears in the wind no more.

Peace is gone, and with it goes the "old hysterical mock disease", vanishing before the shout of "a loyal people shouting a battle-cry". Let the phantom go or stay, cries the hero of the poem—

> Let it go or stay, so I wake to the higher aims
> Of a land that has lost for a little her lust of gold,
> And love of a peace that was full of wrongs and shames,
> Horrible, hateful, monstrous, not to be told;
> And hail once more to the banner of battle unroll'd!

The bitter feeling that was excited by such passages may be gathered from Mr. Gladstone's fierce declamation against them. History will perhaps scarce justify the Crimean War; but Tennyson's view of our national obligations and national interest is the one that has prevailed. Nor was it merely upon the question of national defences that he stood far in front of the trend of thought; at the very height of what we now call the Little England policy, he spoke strongly for maintaining in its fulness our Empire with all its greatness and all its charges. The lines in his "Epilogue to the Queen" which close the *Idylls* found a grateful echo in Canada, and in all probability went far to undo the mischief made by short-sighted statesmen. Written now, they would be a superb summary of our national hopes and aspirations; written as they were in 1872, they showed a mind touched with the spirit of prophetic interpretation:

> And that true North, whereof we lately heard
> A strain to shame us "keep you to yourselves;
> So loyal is too costly! friends—your love
> Is but a burthen: loose the bond, and go".
> Is this the tone of empire? here the faith
> That made us rulers? this, indeed, her voice
> And meaning, whom the roar of Hougoumont
> Left mightiest of all peoples under heaven?
> What shock has fool'd her since, that she should speak
> So feebly? wealthier—wealthier—hour by hour;
> The voice of Britain, or a sinking land,
> Some third-rate isle half-lost among her seas?
> *There* rang her voice, when the full city peal'd
> Thee and thy Prince! The loyal to their crown
> Are loyal to their own far sons, who love
> Our ocean-empire with her boundless homes
> For ever-broadening England, and her throne
> In our vast Orient, and one isle, one isle,
> That knows not her own greatness: if she knows
> And dreads it we are fall'n.

These lines, fine as they are, cannot compare in literary quality with Matthew Arnold's famous passage about the "weary Titan". But, given the conception which Tennyson undoubtedly held, that a poet's first excellence is to be measured by the value of his inspiration to his people, there can be no question which utterance of the two is the more bracing. One cannot class *The Defence of Lucknow* high as poetry; of the Songs, *Hands all Round* and *Riflemen form*, considered as literature the less said the better; and the lines entitled *The Fleet*, which were published in *The Times* in 1886—

> Her fleet is in your hands,
> And in her fleet her Fate—

simply give the impression of a man so angry in
his passion that he is scarcely articulate. But considering all these things together, and the times at
which they were written, it can scarcely be denied
that Tennyson used his poetic gift, and the hold
which it gave him on the feelings of his countrymen, not merely with a high sense of his moral
mission, but with a singularly wide political forecast. Man of peace as he was, he poured iron into
the hearts of his race. A poet can only give of
what is in himself, and his achievement in this
respect ranks him above the artist, who merely
makes life more beautiful and pleasant. As he
has himself put it with his accustomed felicity in
the Epilogue to his battle pieces:

> the Singer for his Art
> Not all in vain may plead
> "The song that nerves a nation's heart
> Is in itself a deed".

Thackeray said that " A. T. was the wisest man
he had ever known ", and I have tried to show by
this series of extracts his sagacity and his power of
getting at the heart of things. For the bearing of
his country as against the world he gave clear
guidance. But when we look to him for political
wisdom in domestic affairs the voice of his answer
is divided.

He went up to Cambridge in 1828, when the
country was in a ferment of revolt against the rule
of privileged classes, against repression of the
democratic spirit; in short, against restrictions
which had been drawn harder than ever since the
horror of the French Revolution and the terror of
Napoleon. The young men of his set, Hallam
and the rest, were full of a generous Liberalism,
and Tennyson, always sensitive to popular aspirations, let himself go with the rest. He had seen

all about him in Lincolnshire terrible signs of the people's discontent—

> When Dives loathed the times and paced his land
>   In fear of worse,
> And sanguine Lazarus felt a vacant hand
>   Fill with *his* purse;

and as he tells, in the dedication to *The Progress of Spring* from which I quote this stanza, had seen one night,

> When thirty ricks,
> All flaming, made an English homestead Hell.

And with the ardour of youth he had believed firmly in the power of Power to remedy injustice. When the news of the Reform Bill's passing reached Somersby in the dead of night, the Tennysons were still living in the rectory as tenants after their father's death. Alfred Tennyson and others of the brothers and sisters "at once sallied out into the darkness and began to ring the church bells madly", to the great confusion and amazement of the parson. And it is this spirit, this *fervor juventæ*, rather than any intensity of love passion, that gives to *Locksley Hall* its high rank among his poems. Nowhere else has he expressed so passionately the poet's feeling for his race—for man, this wonderful creature who year by year wins to himself new forces, gains new conquest over the resistance of things:

> Men, my brothers, men the workers, ever reaping something new:
> That which they have done but earnest of the things that they
>   shall do.

And so he follows the imaginative vision of their future, heaping upon them strange riches, fought for in strange contests with strange engines of

H

death, till the end is peace and order in the "federation of the world".

> There the common sense of most shall hold a fretful realm in awe,
> And the kindly earth shall slumber, lapt in universal law.

Nakedly stated, this is the ideal of universal peace under a cosmopolitan democracy—the millennium of Socialism—and Tennyson was neither cosmopolitan nor a democrat. Every fibre of his nature revolted, when you came to test him, against the ideal implied in either of those words. And already he saw the grimmer side of democratic aspirations, the aspiration of "sanguine Lazarus" after another's purse, and he set it down in a marvellous couplet—

> Slowly comes a hungry people, as a lion creeping nigher,
> Glares at one that nods and winks behind a slowly-dying fire.

But for the moment the tide of enthusiasm swept him away from the deeper instincts of his nature. He believed, with all his heart, in the increasing purpose that ran through the ages; and, for the moment, he was well content to identify that with the march of what we call civilization, and the growing triumphs of machinery.

> Not in vain the distance beacons.   Forward, forward let us range!
> Let the great world spin for ever down the ringing grooves of change!

Is it not significant to read, as we do in the *Life*, that this last line was written after a railway journey from Liverpool, when the rail was as yet so new a thing that Tennyson believed the wheels to run in a groove? And when one thinks of the results accomplished, so great and yet so little, by the marvellous developments since these first days of steam, is it wonderful that we should turn to

Locksley Hall Sixty Years After and find there
what we do find? The fervour of youth has departed, the brain is chilled with age, the contagious
enthusiasm of others has disappeared, the wonders
of machinery, grown commonplace, can no longer
intoxicate, and we find a voice coming from the
man's fundamental instincts. The child of many
generations who have belonged to the governors
rather than to the governed, the man accustomed
by inheritance to be looked up to, to direct rather
than to be directed, speaks, or rather passionately
cries out, against the revolt from all the old discipline, the disappearance of old subordinations. He
has no faith in the great experiments everywhere
being tried about him, and he recedes explicitly
from his youthful profession of faith:

"Forward" rang the voices then, and of the many mine was
one.
Let us hush this cry of "Forward" till ten thousand years have
gone.

There is in all this the natural transition from
youth's standpoint to that of age; and if one is to
weigh the two opinions, allowance must be made
in each for the bias of nature. "When the old
man says," writes Stevenson in his essay, *Crabbed
Age and Youth*, "'Ah, so I thought when I was
your age', he has proved the youth's case. Doubtless, whether from growth of experience or decline
of animal heat, he thinks so no longer; but he
thought so while he was young; and all men
have thought so while they were young, since
there was dew in the morning or hawthorn in
May; and here is another young man adding his
vote to those of previous generations and rivetting
another link to the chain of testimony." An appeal lies from Tennyson in youth to Tennyson
in age; another, not less valid, from the mind of

eighty to the mind of twenty-four. But there is
more in the discrepancy than this merely natural
difference. The real Tennyson, who was, if you
like, a Liberal but no democrat, no real believer in
modern progress, spoke in *The Princess*. Compared with the conservative principles of the day
in which it was written, that poem preached a
creed of advanced liberalism; compared with the
facts of the case, it merely inculcated a healthy
conservatism, a respect for nature. But *Locksley
Hall* is on a different level. The cry of "Forward"
meant something not really in Tennyson's nature.
For once in a way he was crying with the pack, led
and not leading; and between the first *Locksley
Hall* and the second all his political preachings
made for a wide-minded desire to preserve the old.
It is curious to contrast the liberalism of his Cambridge days, and the bell-ringing over Reform Bills,
with his later forecast of what Arthur Hallam might
have been—

> A life in civic action warm,
>   A soul on highest mission sent,
>   A potent voice of Parliament,
> A pillar stedfast in the storm,
>
> Should licensed boldness gather force,
>   Becoming, when the time has birth,
>   A lever to uplift the earth
> And roll it in another course,
>
> With thousand shocks that come and go,
>   With agonies, with energies,
>   With overthrowings, and with cries,
> And undulations to and fro.

This is no jubilant mood in which to contemplate
the cry of "Forward" and its outcome. It is an
early intimation of that dread and hatred of revolution which gradually increased upon the poet, and
of his deep-seated distrust of the undisciplined
masses. He was not the only one who had counted

rashly upon tapping a reservoir of political virtue
in the heart of the working-man; Mill showed the
same faith in his earlier writings, and in the *Representative Government* we find him busy devising
checks by which to safeguard society against the
preponderance of this same factor in it. The lines
To the Duke of Argyll show the real Tennyson, to
whom the true statesman is, like Virgil's *virum
pietate gravem*, one calming from a great moral
height the tumult of a rabble—

> O Patriot Statesman, be thou wise to know
> The limits of resistance, and the bounds
> Determining concession; still be bold
> Not only to slight praise but suffer scorn;
> And be thy heart a fortress to maintain
> The day against the moment, and the year
> Against the day; thy voice, a music heard
> Thro' all the yells and counter-yells of feud
> And faction, and thy will, a power to make
> This ever-changing world of circumstance,
> In changing, chime with never-changing Law.

Law; that is the key-note of Tennyson's teaching
both in politics and morals; that is the truth which
he laboured in his *Idylls* to enforce. In so early a
work as *Œnone* he formulated it; the counsel of
Pallas to Paris condensed into a few pregnant lines
the whole of his philosophy of conduct. "Self-
reverence, self-knowledge, self-control", all imply
submission to a law with which we should identify
ourselves, "Acting the law we live by without
fear".

The spirit of discipline is to him by far more
important than the spirit of unchartered freedom.
Arthur comes as a reformer, but he comes to bring
law. He sweeps away the forests, letting in light;
he tramples out the wild unbridled life of the beasts,
and of men as wild as they; and he establishes the
freedom of an ordered state. He breaks in his sub-

jects and he makes them move, as Duke William in *Harold* aspires to make the "jarring earldoms" of Britain move, "to music and to order". Repression is of the essence of this law which rules everywhere, in man and in the commonwealth; and that is scarcely the ideal of democracy, or even of liberalism. In a fine essay written many years ago Professor Dowden contrasted Tennyson's worship of law with Browning's glorification of impulse, "this or that poor impulse which for once had play unstifled". What has been so well said there, I need not say over again; but it is worth pointing out how Tennyson's morals interpenetrate his views of government. Looseness of any sort makes against discipline; and probably no man has ever stated so strongly the demoralizing effect of sexual irregularities. The Round Table and the whole order which it stands for are based upon chastity, that is, single-hearted love between man and woman; the break-up of that order begins with the first seeds of unlawful love. When men cease to "love one woman only and to cleave to her" they lose faith to God and faith to their king; from this law-breaking spring all other breaches of law. The thing is put as a symbol in the *Idylls*; but in the later poem of *Locksley Hall Sixty Years After*, the fiercest of all the fierce denunciations is directed against the growing license of literature—

Authors—essayist, atheist, novelist, realist, rhymester, play your part,
Paint the mortal shame of nature with the living hues of Art.

Rip your brothers' vices open, strip your own foul passions bare,
Down with Reticence, down with Reverence,—forward—naked —let them stare.

Feed the budding rose of boyhood with the drainage of your sewer,
Send the drain into the fountain, lest the stream should issue pure.

Set the maiden fancies wallowing in the troughs of Zolaism,—
Forward, forward, ay and backward, downward too into the
abysm.

Do your best to charm the worst, to lower the rising race of
men;
Have we risen from out the beast, then back into the beast again?

That is what caps the climax; that is the worst
feature that Tennyson sees in the modern life which
he denounces with all the bitterness of disappoint-
ment. There is, however, no want of other accusa-
tion; the maiming of brute beasts, dynamite and
revolver, "menace, madness, spoken lies"; lies
of democracy, equalizing the unequal, seeking
upon matters of imperial import "the suffrage of
the plough"; ruling the simple masses through
the cunning of words.

So the Higher wields the Lower, while the Lower is the Higher.

Never was there a fiercer rhetoric of denunciation—

Chaos, Cosmos! Cosmos, Chaos! once again the sickening
game;
Freedom, free to slay herself, and dying while they shout her
name.

Step by step we gain'd a freedom known to Europe, known to
all;
Step by step we rose to greatness,—thro' the tonguesters we may
fall.

You that woo the Voices—tell them "Old Experience is a fool",
Teach your flatter'd kings that only those who cannot read can
rule.

Pluck the mighty from their seat, but set no meek ones in their
place;
Pillory Wisdom in your markets, pelt your offal at her face.

Tumble Nature heel o'er head, and, yelling with the yelling
street,
Set the feet above the brain and swear the brain is in the feet.

This is the very madness of reaction, and any fair-minded person looking at the indictment will allow that it does not correspond with facts. And indeed neither of the *Locksley Hall* poems is to be taken as fitly representative of Tennyson's mind. Each poem has in it a fire, almost a frenzy, that sets it apart from the rest of his work, or rather in a class with the rhapsodies that open and close *Maud*; and each, with all the marvel of its eloquence, is marred by a sort of falsetto note. The voice rises almost to a shriek. For Tennyson's real mind upon politics I would look rather to the poems, calm in their balance of phrasing and their stately self-contained measure, which praise the equipoise of the constitution, and the freedom which restrains—

> Loather of the lawless crown
> As of the lawless crowd.

And if one compares the later and less-known poem on *Freedom* from which I quote these lines with the magnificent stanzas written half a century earlier, one sees a perfect harmony of thought—the same love of fearless truth, the same hatred of "the falsehood of extremes". Nothing is gone but the dew of the morning; and with that is vanished perhaps also something of the triumphant confidence in truth, something of the unalloyed pride in the English race; and instead there lurk in the background sombre apprehensions. As Tennyson grew older he began to be haunted by a new thought, instilled into him with the teachings of science; that if selection and progress was everywhere in nature, so also were degeneration and decadence; and he watched with anxious, unavailing eyes for a sign of a backward swing of the pendulum—for

> Reversion, ever dragging Evolution in the mud.

He saw it plainly there in Paris, and his minute scrutiny for signs of it in England blinded him, I think, to the more hopeful features in the political and social order. But politics are not like religion; they cannot be fairly studied in retreat; and the utterances of a man who lived in voluntary seclusion from the movement of affairs, judging acts and actors from a distance, can never be regarded as trustworthy guides. In the rub and bustle of affairs men learn tolerance. Your recluse, like Carlyle, is apt to fulminate damnation against what is merely distasteful to his own prepossessions.

Chapter VI.

Tennyson s Outlook upon Nature.

I have tried to show that Tennyson's whole conception of the spiritual universe was profoundly coloured by the evolutionist theory. Not in this matter alone, but in his outlook upon life and the physical world, he sees and thinks and speaks like a poet who is also a man of science. The truths of astronomy are for ever present to his mind, not as mere formulæ, but realized with all the intensity of a poet's imagination. Against the claim of man to spiritual significance he is for ever setting man's physical insignificance. One finds it first in *The Two Voices*:

> I said, "When first the world began,
> Young Nature thro' five cycles ran,
> And in the sixth she moulded man.
>
> "She gave him mind, the lordliest
> Proportion, and, above the rest,
> Dominion in the head and breast."

Thereto the silent voice replied;
" Self-blinded are you by your pride:
Look up thro' night: the world is wide.

" This truth within thy mind rehearse,
That in a boundless universe
Is boundless better, boundless worse.

" Think you this mould of hopes and fears
Could find no statelier than his peers
In yonder hundred million spheres?"

And the same thought is put with far more power
in *Vastness*:

Many a hearth upon our dark globe sighs after many a vanish'd
face,
Many a planet by many a sun may roll with the dust of a
vanish'd race.

Raving politics, never at rest—as this poor earth's pale history
runs,—
What is it all but a trouble of ants in the gleam of a million
million of suns?

In *Despair*, the tragedy of creation that "groaneth
and travaileth in pain" extends far beyond human
ken:

And the suns of the limitless Universe sparkled and shone in
the sky,
Flashing with fires as of God, but we knew that their light was
a lie—
Bright as with deathless hope—but, however they sparkled and
shone,
The dark little worlds running round them were worlds of woe
like our own—
No soul in the heaven above, no soul on the earth below,
A fiery scroll written over with lamentation and woe.

But by far the finest example of an imagination fed
with the facts of astronomy is in a really great
passage of *Locksley Hall Sixty Years After*, where
the poet takes up from the earlier poem the theme
of a warless earth which his young mind held in

vision, and comments upon it with the experience of a life. Sixty years has seen the reign of science, and how much nearer are we to the vision? "Warless earth", he cries—

Warless? when her tens are thousands, and her thousands millions, then—
All her harvest all too narrow—who can fancy warless men?

Warless? War will die out late then. Will it ever? late or soon?
Can it, till this outworn earth be dead as yon dead world the moon?

Life on the moon is dead, the new astronomy tells us, worn out in anguish; but across the worlds who knows of that anguish? From across space that theatre of desolation looks a perpetual peace. And then, by a noble reach of thought, he shows us the littleness of our own destiny—"the trouble of ants" —that, seen across space, may look like utter tranquillity:

Dead, but how her living glory lights the hall, the dune, the grass!
Yet the moonlight is the sunlight, and the sun himself will pass.

Venus near her! smiling downward at this earthlier earth of ours,
Closer on the Sun, perhaps a world of never-fading flowers.

Hesper, whom the poet call'd the Bringer home of all good things.
All good things may move in Hesper, perfect peoples, perfect kings.

Hesper—Venus—were we native to that splendour or in Mars,
We should see the Globe we groan in, fairest of their evening stars.

Could we dream of wars and carnage, craft and madness, lust and spite,
Roaring London, raving Paris, in that point of peaceful light?

Might we not in glancing heavenward on a star so silver-fair,
Yearn, and clasp the hands and murmur, "Would to God that we were there"?

Two things there are, said Kant, that fill me with awe: the starry heaven above me and the moral law within me. That is for Tennyson also the lesson of astronomy; the permanent contrast between man's pettiness in the universe and his "far-off touch of greatness", for the poem closes, as I have already urged, with an emphatic assertion of man's eternal destiny.

Another such contrast is that between the law of love in which man's heart finds the key-note of the universe and the law of cruelty which we see everywhere in Nature.

For nature is one with rapine, a harm no preacher can heal;
The May-fly is torn by the swallow, the sparrow spear'd by the shrike,
And the whole little wood where I sit is a world of plunder and prey.

There is the fact stated; but for the contrast expressed one has to turn to a passage of *In Memoriam* that may rank among the noblest in English verse. Here in a few lines the poem concentrates the whole existence of man hoping against hope—"who built him fanes of *fruitless* prayer"—and the attitude of nature ranged in permanent denial of all his beliefs:

And he, shall he,

Man, her last work, who seem'd so fair,
    Such splendid purpose in his eyes,
    Who roll'd the psalm to wintry skies,
Who built him fanes of fruitless prayer,

Who trusted God was love indeed
    And love Creation's final law—
    Tho' Nature, red in tooth and claw
With ravine, shriek'd against his creed—

Who loved, who suffer'd countless ills,
    Who battled for the True, the Just,
    Be blown about the desert dust,
Or seal'd within the iron hills?

These appear to me the two main lessons which
Tennyson learnt from science; from astronomy
man's insignificance in space, from geology his
transitoriness in time.   It is hardly necessary to
prove from casual references how fully his mind was
fed with the facts of science. Such a passage as
this from *The Two Voices* proves a knowledge
which no other English poet had cared to acquire:

> Before the little ducts began
> To feed thy bones with lime, and ran
> Their course, till thou wert also man.

It is also an example of that extraordinary power
which Tennyson repeatedly displayed—the power
of clothing the teachings of science in a style that
gave them beauty and hid nothing of their clearness.
Lucretius is among his finest poems; it is also
perhaps the best concise statement ever written of
the atomic theory of creation; and a few lines of
Lady Psyche's lecture in *The Princess* condense a
more modern view of the same. It is easy also
to detect the skill with which Tennyson used his
knowledge to realize physically in our minds things
that to most of us are only abstract knowledge.
For instance, in the lines—

> Move eastward, happy earth, and leave
>   Yon orange sunset waning slow:
> From fringes of the faded eve,
>   O, happy planet, eastward go;
> Till over thy dark shoulder glow
>   Thy silver sister-world, and rise
>   To glass herself in dewy eyes
> That watch me from the glen below.
>
> Ah, bear me with thee, smoothly borne,
>   Dip forward under starry light,
> And move me to my marriage-morn,
>   And round again to happy night.

A fine image too is latent under what seems a

commonplace in the lines in memory of the Prince
Consort addressed to the Queen:

> Her—over all whose realms, to their last isle
> Commingled with the gloom of imminent war,
> The shadow of his loss drew like eclipse,
> Darkening the world.

For what is pictured is not merely gloom, but a
gloom that swept round the world swift as the
electric message could leap from point to point;
literally, like the shadow round the spinning globe.
Everything, all knowledge, with Tennyson went to
feed the visual imagination; he was before all
things a creator of forms.   In his observation of
nature one feels the trained eye of the sportsman or
artist, but also the disciplined observation of the
botanist or geologist. He saw with extraordinary
distinctness, as I shall have to show, all that was
about him; but he could also construct, with almost
equal vividness, imaginary landscape from description.   His mind revelled in tropical imaginings;
there is a story in the *Life* of his disgust because
he could not kindle Wordsworth's enthusiasm with
an account of some island in the South Seas where
Spring came with a flush of crimson leafage.
There is no need to quote the famous passage in
Locksley Hall that describes

> Summer isles of Eden lying in dark purple spheres of sea.

In the poem called *The Voyage* there is a succession
of landscapes like those in *The Lotos-Eaters*, but
based on fact:

> By sands and steaming flats and floods
>   Of mighty mouth we scudded fast,
> And hills and scarlet-mingled woods
>   Glow'd for a moment as we passed.

But the most notable of these must at least be

quoted—the great passage in *Enoch Arden*, which has been praised almost without measure, but scarcely beyond its deserts.

> The mountain wooded to the peak, the lawns
> And winding glades high up like ways to Heaven,
> The slender coco's drooping crown of plumes,
> The lightning flash of insect and of bird,
> The lustre of the long convolvuluses
> That coiled around the stately stems, and ran
> Ev'n to the limit of the land, the glows
> And glories of the broad belt of the world,
> All these he saw; but what he fain had seen
> He could not see, the kindly human face,
> Nor ever hear a kindly voice, but heard
> The myriad shriek of wheeling ocean-fowl,
> The league-long roller thundering on the reef,
> The moving whisper of huge trees that branch'd
> And blossom'd in the zenith, or the sweep
> Of some precipitous rivulet to the wave,
> As down the shore he ranged, or all day long
> Sat often in the seaward-gazing gorge,
> A shipwreck'd sailor, waiting for a sail:
> No sail from day to day, but every day
> The sunrise broken into scarlet shafts
> Among the palms and ferns and precipices;
> The blaze upon the waters to the east;
> The blaze upon his island overhead;
> The blaze upon the waters to the west;
> Then the great stars that globed themselves in Heaven,
> The hollower-bellowing ocean, and again,
> The scarlet shafts of sunrise—but no sail.

The teachings of science thus had a double importance in Tennyson's development. Upon them first of all was based his whole attitude towards religion and the universe. He accepted resolutely and unflinchingly all that science could prove; but by reason of his close acquaintance with what was then accounted the enemy, he saw also the limitations of this dreaded power. Seeing what it could prove and explain, he saw also what it could neither prove nor explain. And secondly, beyond this

abstract intellectual framework which Science provided for his thought, it furnished also the most
fertile food for his imagination. Child of his age
in this, as in all else, he wondered at the marvels
of his own generation; and not less instinct with
beauty to him than either man or woman, picture
or poem, were "the fairy tales of Science and the
long result of time". The tale of man's victories
over nature filled him with pride; but Science was
more to him than a recital of discoveries, or of such
exploits as Mr. Kipling delights to celebrate. It
gave a new beauty and significance to what was
already beautiful. One cannot rightly separate
Tennyson's observation of Nature from his interest
in physical science. He looked at Nature with the
eyes of a lover awake to every loveliness, from the
dimness of far-off hills to the delicate markings of
a tiny flower at his feet; but he always looked with
the eyes of one trained in the school of Science.
He has been compared to Wordsworth, and judged
inferior because he did not attempt, as Wordsworth
did, to find a living spirit, a conscious face, in
mountains and rivers: the judgment seems to me
wholly unreasonable. Man was in Tennyson's eye
the roof and crown of things; the interpreter of
Nature, whose forces he moulded to his own will;
her master and not her dependant. Nature was
only the setting for man, the material given on
which he might display his energies, the record in
which he might read, if he could, his fate. Nature
would answer his moods; sunlight to Mariana in
the South might show only desolation; but Nature
could only give back an echo, or at most answer
when she was questioned. The other view was
native to Wordsworth, and true no doubt for him;
but Tennyson's appears to be the saner and more
genuine, and his observation infinitely finer and
more searching. It would, I think, be hard to

establish that Wordsworth really observed with
any exceptional closeness, though he certainly introduced into poetry a new use of detail. The
magic of sights and sounds in lonely places; the
cuckoo's cry

> Breaking the silence of the seas
> Among the farthest Hebrides;

he has rendered incomparably, and that sense of
exaltation which mountain air only can give. But,
as an observer of Nature, and as a painter of her
innumerable aspects great and small, Tennyson
goes far beyond Wordsworth or any poet since
Shakespeare.

The closeness of study upon which his most
gorgeous pictures rested,—comparable to the work
of Turner — redeems even the affectation of his
juvenile pieces. For the most part the landscape
in them is vague and conventional; diamond ril-
lets, gleaming fountains, green lawns and sighing
breezes.

> From the green rivage many a fall
> Of diamond rillets musical,
> Thro' little crystal arches low
> Down from the central fountain's flow
> Fall'n silver-chiming, seemed to shake
> The sparkling flints beneath the prow.

But if you come to study the Juvenilia close, you
see again and again the truth of imagination. It
is an imagination nursed in a land of willow and
poplar, a land of plains—

> grassy, wild, and bare,
> Wide, wild, and open to the air.

fenced from the sea by sand-hills. Nothing can be
juster in observation than the lines in the *Ode to
Memory* (written at about fifteen) which first re-

vealed to Mr. Leslie Stephen (by his own account)
the charm of fen scenery.

> Whether the high field on the bushless Pike,
>   Or even a sand-built ridge
> Of heaped hills that mound the sea,
> Overblown with murmurs harsh,
>   Or even a lowly cottage whence we see
> Stretch'd wide and wild the waste enormous marsh,
>   Where from the frequent bridge,
>   Like emblems of infinity,
> The trenched waters run from sky to sky.

You feel, too, in the *Song* which describes the spirit
of autumn a mind in the very closest touch with
what it pictures: the "moist rich smell of the rot-
ting leaves", and the first signs of decay when the
strong sunflower grows heavy-headed, and the
petals lose their lustre.

And, finally, the one poem among the Juvenilia
which has always to be seriously considered is
Mariana, essentially a piece of imaginative landscape; landscape seen through a veil of human
passion, but seen with the keenest intensity of
vision.   One need only recall the opening:

> With blackest moss the flower-plots
>   Were thickly crusted, one and all:
> The rusted nails fell from the knots
>   That held the pear to the gable-wall.

These are Virgil's *loca senta situ*, but seen how
definitely! how admirable is that touch, so minute,
yet so ample in suggestion of the neglected garden
where the trees hang loose from the wall!

And everywhere one comes upon the characteristic that never left Tennyson, his delight in all
the shapes and sounds of water.   He tells you here
in his early poems of

> The sea
> At midnight when the crisp slope waves,
> After a tempest, rib and fret
> The broad imbased beach;

he tells you of

> the brook that loves
> To purl o'er matted cress and ribbed sand,
> Or dimple in the dark of rushy coves,
> Drawing into his narrow earthen urn,
>   In every elbow and turn,
> The filter'd tribute of the rough woodland.

There is not yet the same breadth and happiness of touch that was to show later how

> Twice a day the Severn fills,
> The salt sea-water passes by,
> And hushes half the babbling Wye,
> And makes a silence in the hills;

nor the skilled magic that, after eighty years of learning, evolved the image of

> Such a tide as moving seems asleep,
>   Too full for sound and foam;

but there is the same study, the same delight. I have named from among the later passages the two that instantly suggest themselves by their supreme beauty; but if one wished to parallel more closely these early sketches, how easy it would be. The Brook has its own poem—though I think that is not the brook that passed

> The seven elms and poplars four
> That stand beside my father's door;

but a brook of livelier runnings than can be found among the Lincolnshire flats; and the sea is never out of Tennyson's verse. One recalls the echoing passage in *Maud*, where the lover walks in his garden and hears the tempestuous voices of wave and beach; one recalls the "Wild wave in the wide North-Sea", with all

> Its stormy crests that smoke against the skies,

to which is likened the charge of Lancelot's kin upon Lancelot unrecognized; and how many other images taken from the sea, whether in storm or calm.

One image which has for me a singular power of suggestion is that in the close of *The Palace of Art* which describes the Soul's punishment, shut for its spiritual exclusive arrogance in "dull stagnation" till it feels like

> A still salt pool, lock'd in with bars of sand,
>   Left on the shore; that hears all night
> The plunging seas draw backward from the land
>   Their moon-led waters white.

And need I quote the longing of the Lotos-eaters

> To watch the crisping ripples on the beach
> And tender curving lines of creamy spray—

where the sound, as always, beautifully answers the sense.

Tennyson made his home by the sea, where in winter—

> the hoary Channel
> Tumbles a billow on chalk and sand,

and where in summer the waves made a "silent sapphire-spangled marriage-ring of the land"; the home of his boyhood was almost within the hearing of a rougher, grayer water, on the bleak east coast; and from the two he learnt all moods of the sea, at least as a landsman knows it. But the rivers of his affection, save for what he saw in the Gorge of Cauteretz and pictured in *Œnone*, were all the rivers of a plain country, not the brown salmon-haunted streams that we know in Ireland and Scotland, which race and break, but rather such as this pictures:

A league of grass washed by a slow broad stream
That, stirr'd with languid pulses of the oar,
Waves all its lazy lilies and creeps on
Barge-laden to three arches of a bridge
Crowned with the minster towers.

His delight was in the earth and its creatures
as well as in the sea and the streams. As one
turns over the poems, on every page there appear
touches of that minute imaginative sight which
comes of observation informed by knowledge. Here
is an instance from *The Two Voices*:

To-day I saw the dragon-fly
Come from the wells where he did lie.

An inner impulse rent the veil
Of his old husk; from head to tail
Came out clear plates of sapphire mail.

He dried his wings: like gauze they grew,
Thro' crofts and pastures wet with dew
A living flash of light he flew.

Tennyson knows how the blackbird, gorged with
summer fruit, ceases his song; he knows how the
"dropping snipe" hums in the dusk; he knows
how plumage changes with the season, and the
lapwing renews his crest with the spring; he knows
how the many-wintered crow is the leader of the
homing rookery; all this lore he shares with the
poacher or gamekeeper. He knows, too, how,
when autumn came, the bracken "rusted on the
crags"; he knows how autumn "lays a fiery finger
on the leaves"; he sees these effects like an artist.
But he sees, too, what many an artist would never
notice; how with spring's coming "rosy plumelets
tuft the larch"; how the poppy comes limp and
crumpled from its sheath; and how the drooping
chestnut buds spread gradually into the perfect fan.
He sees in short like the artist or the collector, but

he sees also like the man of science. He knows the loves of the plants; he can realize

> These blind motions of the Spring
> That show the year is turned;

that bid the oak to

> languidly adjust
> His vapid vegetable loves
> With anthers and with dust.

How curiously minute is his accuracy I can best prove by quoting at some length from Mr. Lowe's work, *The Yew Trees of Great Britain and Ireland.*

"In the poems of Lord Tennyson, and especially in *In Memoriam*, the yew is frequently mentioned with that minute and accurate observation in which he transcends all other poets. But he, the truest interpreter of Nature in all her aspects, has not escaped the tendency to regard the tree in its gloomy aspect, as being associated with the cemetery. This was to be expected in such a poem as *In Memoriam*; but how beautiful are some of the touches with which he depicts it! Thus in Stanza II., beginning at 'Old Yew, which graspest at the stones', he goes on to say:

> The seasons bring the flower again,
> And bring the firstling to the flock;
> And in the dusk of thee, the clock
> Beats out the little lives of men.
>
> O not for thee the glow, the bloom,
> Who changest not in any gale,
> Nor branding summer suns avail
> To touch thy thousand years of gloom:
>
> And gazing on thee, sullen tree,
> Sick for thy stubborn hardihood,
> I seem to fail from out my blood
> And grow incorporate into thee.

It has been supposed by some that Tennyson in this stanza implies that the yew does not flower, and that

his later alteration in the eleventh edition is a confession
of his error; but it is inconceivable that so minute an
observer, who in another place speaks of the fruit, can
have been so ignorant as to suppose that the tree does
not flower. He evidently intended that it had not conspicuous and brilliant flowers. 'O, not for thee the
glow, the *bloom*;' but he never could have meant to say
that it had no flower.

"In the later edition, he makes a change from 'the
thousand years of gloom' and points out that even the
yew has its 'golden hour' which had been lacking to
the subject of the poem:

> And answering now my random stroke
> With fruitful cloud and living smoke—
>
> To thee too comes the golden hour
> When flower is *feeling after flower*.

The difficulty which has beset the general reader is in
great measure caused by overlooking the diœcious habit
of the tree; the pollen being on one tree and the berry
on the other. . . .

"It is very possible that Lord Tennyson felt that the
original lines seemed to imply an absence of flower in
the yew, and hence the alteration to make his meaning
more obvious.

"The alteration in Canto xxxix. runs as follows:

> Old warder of these buried bones,
> And answering now my random stroke
> With fruitful cloud and living smoke,
> Dark yew, that graspest at the stones
>
> And dippest towards the dreamless head,
> To thee too comes the golden hour
> When flower is feeling after flower
> But Sorrow—fixt upon the dead,
>
> And darkening the dark graves of men,—
> What whisper'd from her lying lips?
> Thy gloom is kindled at the tips[1]
> And passes into gloom again.

[1] The young shoots in spring being a brighter green and becoming darker
with age.

" We find the same smoke-like dust doing duty again in *The Holy Grail* (line 13):

> Beneath a world-old yew-tree, darkening half
> The cloisters, on a gustful April morn
> That puff'd the swaying branches into smoke.

It is the pollen arising in clouds from the staminal flowers of the tree which appears as smoke—'living smoke' Tennyson truly calls it."

As another example of this curious and learned observation I am tempted to point out how Tennyson seems to have been enamoured of a familiar prettiness in a weed. He first uses the dandelion for a symbolism in *The Poet*, telling how the singer's " vagrant melodies " flew abroad on the winds at random till they lighted.

> Then, like the arrow-seeds of the field flower,
>   The fruitful wit
>
> Cleaving, took root, and springing forth anew
>   Where'er they fell, behold,
> Like to the mother plant in semblance, grew
>   A flower all gold.

The dandelion comes again in the *Idylls*, for the Sun's shield with its golden blazon flares upon Gareth like

> the flower
> That blows a globe of after arrowlets;

and in *Aylmer's Field* the same image closes a pretty passage which describes how the two lovers, still children, played together, and Leolin

> told her fairy-tales,
> Show'd her the fairy footings on the grass,
> The little dells of cowslip, fairy palms,
> The pretty marestail forest, fairy pines,
> Or from the tiny pitted target blew
> What look'd a flight of fairy arrows aim'd
> All at one mark, all hitting.

It would be tedious to multiply instances of this minute study of flowers, which can only be paralleled in the poetry of the man who wrote in *Cymbeline* of the mole on Imogen's breast:

> cinque-spotted like the crimson drops
> I' the bottom of a cowslip.

But it should be observed with what skill and what love Tennyson has rendered the common beauties of rich English country.   The last of his pictures in *The Palace of Art* is sketched in the quatrain that every one knows describing the English home, "a haunt of ancient peace"; and it is from the *English Idyls* that one may best illustrate his talent for rendering, not so much the Turneresque haze in which he bathed so many of his visions, especially those drawn from classical mythology, as the nearer details.   One goes to them for foregrounds, not for distances.   What could be more charming or more complete than the picture given here:

> I loved the brimming wave that swam
>   Thro' quiet meadows round the mill,
> The sleepy pool above the dam,
>   The pool beneath it never still,
> The meal-sacks on the whiten'd floor,
>   The dark round of the dripping wheel,
> The very air about the door
>   Made misty with the floating meal.

The last touch offended the susceptibilities of Lockhart, but in this instance Tennyson was wisely resolute; and in *Enoch Arden* he does not shrink from representing Philip

> like the working bee in blossom-dust,
> Blanch'd with his mill.

One could quote beautiful touches of observation indefinitely from these *English Idyls*; for instance, in *The Brook* the picture of the boy lover "like a wader in the surf", who comes "waist-deep in meadow-sweet". But it is in *Aylmer's Field* that they cluster thickest—the Idyl that is laid in a land of "hops and poppy-mingled corn"; the tale of Edith Aylmer and her fair-haired lover whose cheek wore

> a but less vivid hue
> Than of that islet in the chestnut bloom;

the tale that pictures the Kentish cottages set each in its own peculiar glory of flowers, as a background to its happy opening; and then the shattered oak which played post for the lovers. What a sense of summer dawn is given in these four lines:

> The father panting woke, and oft, as dawn
> Aroused the black republic on his elms,
> Sweeping the frothfly from the fescue, brush'd
> Thro' the dim meadow toward his treasure-trove.

Elsewhere, it may be noticed, Tennyson uses the motions of a rookery to mark the hour, at the close of *The Princess*:—

> a shout arose again and made
> The long line of the approaching rookery swerve
> From the elms and shook the branches of the deer
> From slope to slope through distant ferns, and rang
> Beyond the bourn of sunset.

The truth of picture-making observation is there; but for a still better example of it I should quote the last lines of *Aylmer's Field*:

> And where the two contrived their daughter's good,
> Lies the hawk's cast, the mole has made his run,
> The hedgehog underneath the plantain bores,
> The rabbit fondles his own harmless face,
> The slow-worm creeps, and the thin weasel there
> Follows the mouse, and all is open field.

Lines like these can only be written by a man who year after year has lain quiet out of doors, motionless, till the pretty brutes came out and played or went about their business all round him.

These illustrations everyone may pursue for himself; but, after all, the point needs no labouring. Most of us remember the passage in *Cranford* where the gentleman farmer takes shame to himself because he has lived all his life in the country, yet never found out that ash buds were black in March till this new poet told him to look at them.   The power of observation, at least in so far as regards tree and flower life, was never carried further, nor ever joined with a more perfect felicity of expression.   And in the larger business of suggesting whole landscapes by a few touches, Tennyson has no master.   His landscape is never put there for its own sake; he never indulges idly in word-painting; it is part and parcel of the story or the thought. This again one could prove by endless quotation, but I need only extract two passages from the *In Memoriam*, whose application to contrasted moods, or rather to moods that succeed as storm follows calm, everyone will remember:

> Calm is the morn without a sound,
>> Calm as to suit a calmer grief,
>> And only thro' the faded leaf
> The chestnut pattering to the ground:
>
> Calm and deep peace on this high wold,
>> And on these dews that drench the furze,
>> And all the silvery gossamers
> That twinkle into green and gold:
>
> Calm and still light on yon great plain
>> That sweeps with all its autumn bowers,
>> And crowded farms and lessening towers,
> To mingle with the bounding main.

The poet has the advantage of the painter in that he can appeal to more senses than one; and it is worth noticing how the very spirit of autumn is caught in the first stanza by the evocation of sound. There is sound too in the companion poem, though a very different sound:

> To-night the winds begin to rise
>   And roar from yonder dropping day:
>   The last red leaf is whirl'd away,
> The rooks are blown about the skies;
>
> The forest crack'd, the waters curl'd,
>   The cattle huddled on the lea;
>   And wildly dash'd on tower and tree
> The sunbeam strikes along the world.

The great masters of landscape painting have been English; but neither Constable nor Turner has felt more finely or rendered more completely the grace or majesty of form, the glow or purity of colour, and the living play of light and shade, than this painter in words, in whom the love of these was so intense that it inspired his art with what is no less than a magic of evocation.

Chapter VII.

The Poems.

Such criticism as the preceding pages contain has been directed primarily to Tennyson's ideas or habits of mind, and I pass now to a general consideration of the poems. Of these the *Idylls*, as has been already shown, appeared to the poet's own generation by far the most important — the consummate achievement of his life. They detach themselves cleanly from the rest of his work, and must be dealt with in a separate chapter. Here

it need only be said, that in my judgment Tennyson will take rank in the eyes of posterity, not
by the *Idylls*, but by *Maud* and *In Memoriam*;
that is, not by his work in narrative, but by the
greatest of his lyrics. *Maud* and *In Memoriam*
are essentially lyrical, not only in form but in
feeling; yet they represent very different aspects of
the poet's nature. *In Memoriam*, with its "short
swallow flights of song", is mainly the poetry of
reflection—of close thought fused by strong emotion into the fire of poetry; *Maud* is first and
foremost a rendering of passion in its different
moods; and such thought as enters into the framework of the poem comes in moments of reaction,
and is tinged deeply with the colour of love.
Probably in all generations men will prefer the
one poem or the other according to their temperament; but it seems to me clear that they rank
in importance above Tennyson's other work. Yet
there are many things among the shorter pieces in
no way inferior to the finest passages in either, and
these also make an integral part of the basis on
which his reputation will rest.

Maud, In Memoriam, The Princess, and the plays
are criticised in some detail elsewhere in the course
of this volume. Before criticising the great mass
of the shorter poems one must attempt some sort of
grouping. A large number of the most important
are in form dramatic monologues, where a character is made to express his or her personality, or tell
a life history in one protracted speech or soliloquy.
Next to these come the *English Idyls*—written for
the most part in blank verse (but occasionally with
songs interspersed)—which are highly wrought
narratives of domestic life. Besides these two
classes there is a mass of poems in rhyme, chiefly
ballads or pure lyrics. In the former sometimes
the narrative element preponderates, as in *The*

Revenge or *The Charge of the Light Brigade*; sometimes the lyrical, as in *The Lady of Shalott* or *Sir Galahad*. The pure lyrics vary from abstract meditations like *Vastness* or *The Higher Pantheism*, or again from the magnificent threnody upon Wellington, to the simplicity of a bird's song. Nor must we forget the occasional poems, such as the addresses to the Queen and other members of the Royal Family, or the letter to F. D. Maurice. Last of all must be placed the verses written *leviore plectro—The Talking Oak, The Day Dream, Will Waterproof*, and the like. The poems in dialect form a class by themselves; they are all humorous dramatic monologues; and one is tempted at the risk of a cross-division to make another separate class of the poems upon subjects drawn from the classical mythology. The Juvenilia I omit from this classification, as they have only a historic and technical interest for posterity, except *The Poet*, which is a fine lyric, and *Mariana*, which belongs properly to a group that I do not know how to describe—except as picture poems.

Criticism naturally directs itself first to the poems upon classical subjects, for in these Tennyson first achieved a masterpiece. *Œnone* and *The Lotos-Eaters*, though not in their consummate form, were included in the volume of 1833. *Ulysses* was written almost directly after the death of Arthur Hallam, and *Tithonus* (though not published till Thackeray begged a poem for the *Cornhill* twenty-five years later) was unearthed from an old note-book of that same date.

It is easy enough to see why Tennyson should have made his first successes here. This was not raw material that he wrought in, but the stuff of poetry handled for three thousand years by poets; old myths already made beautiful, yet pregnant for every man with a fresh significance. *Ulysses* is true to the temper of the Ithacan as we know him in Homer; but it was written to express the poet's own revolt against despondency after the death of his friend. There is no need to quote what everyone knows by heart; but I cannot imagine an age which should be indifferent to *Ulysses*. It is for all ages; but stamped with the impress of a period in which intellectual adventure was rife, an age of discovery.

> I am a part of all that I have met;
> Yet all experience is an arch wherethro'
> Gleams that untravell'd world, whose margin fades
> For ever and for ever when I move.

Œnone is hardly less perfect; it is essentially a poem of description as *Ulysses* is of character. Yet, just as in the end of *Ulysses* you find one of Tennyson's finest landscape effects, so in *Œnone* you find the completest expression—in the speech of Pallas—that Tennyson ever gave to his moral code. The motive which most stirred his spirit— the hope of a future life—was out of place when his scene was laid among the Greeks; but his worship of law could nowhere more fitly be expressed. Yet the spirit of the poem is not Greek: it recalls indeed the Sicilian Muse of Theocritus, but far more closely the narrative style of Virgil in his *Georgics* or *Eclogues*.

Tithonus, again, is a Greek story, but not treated in the classic spirit. In most of the Greek or Roman references to the legend Tithonus is immortal and immortally young; nowhere is this tragedy of "immortal age beside immortal youth" insisted on. And it is strange and characteristic that Tennyson should have been content to tell the story merely as a story, with no suggestion of any symbolism. All that he cares for is to give the picture; to keep all the beauty and the pathos, and avoid every touch of ugliness in this miracle of high-wrought style. There is an obvious parallel in Mr. Stephen Phillips's beautiful *Marpessa*, which tells of the choice made by a girl, who, being wooed by the sun-god, prefers a mortal lover. She chooses the human heritage of sorrow, the human delight of children, rather than to be like Apollo, "a spirit gliding through tranquillity". But the more instructive contrast is with a great work of prose imagination. The tragedy of *Tithonus* is the same as that of the Struldbrugs in a terrible passage of *Gulliver's Travels*. It is worth quoting the latter to show in how different manner the same thought—that life protracted without corresponding youth—may strike two minds.

"After this preface he gave me a particular account of the Struldbrugs among them. He said, they commonly acted like mortals, till about thirty years old; after which by degrees they grew melancholy and dejected, increasing in both till they came to fourscore. This he learned from their own confessions; for otherwise, there not being above two or three of that species born in an age, they were too few to form a general observation by. When they came to fourscore years, which is reckoned the extremity of living in this country, they had not only all the follies and infirmities of other old men, but many more, which arose from the dreadful prospect of never dying. They were not only opinionative, peevish, covetous, morose, vain, talkative, but incapable of friendship, and dead to all natural affection, which never descended below their grandchildren. Envy and impotent desires are their prevailing passions. But those objects against which their envy seems principally directed, are the vices of the younger sort, and the deaths of the old. By reflecting on the former, they find themselves cut off from all possibility of pleasure; and whenever they see a funeral they lament and repine that others are gone to a harbour of rest, to which they themselves never can hope to arrive. They have no remembrance of anything, but what they learned and observed in their youth and middle age, and even that is very imperfect. And for the truth or particulars of any fact, it is safer to depend on common tradition than upon their best recollections. The least miserable among them appear to be those who turn to dotage, and entirely lose their memories; these meet with more pity and assistance, because they want many bad qualities which abound in others.

"If a Struldbrug happen to marry one of his own kind, the marriage is dissolved of course by the courtesy of the kingdom, as soon as the younger of the two comes to be fourscore. For the law thinks it a reasonable indulgence, that those who are condemned without any fault of their own to a perpetual continuance in the world, should not have their misery doubled by the load of a wife."

Tithonus, it need hardly be said, mourns also for the passion that can no longer touch him, and envies the "happy men that have the power to die". I have not quoted the repulsive physical traits on which Swift dwells: but the contrast is strange indeed between them and the superb lines that lament over "this grey shadow once a man", yet, in describing his gradual wreckage at the hands of the "strong Hours", suggest only a dignity like that of withered oak trees. But the poem can scarcely rank with *Œnone* and *Ulysses*, for the simple reason that it is a masterpiece of style and nothing beyond that. *Œnone* tells a human passion; *Ulysses* puts into imperishable words an aspiration as old as man, and growing stronger with every century of his development. It was probably some consciousness of this deficiency in *Tithonus* that led Tennyson to suppress it for so long; yet it is a deficiency that we do not care to dwell on. Beauty is not so common that we need ask it always to be more than beauty.

Three other poems in the same class, though of

a very different rank, are *Tiresias, Demeter and Persephone*, and *The Death of Œnone*. Of these we need only say that they are better than the best imitations of Tennyson published by Sir Lewis Morris and the rest—*Demeter* vastly better. *Godiva*, though it is on an English subject, is classical in treatment. This, like *The Death of Œnone*, is a simple narration, not a monologue. The poems on Sir John Oldcastle and that on Columbus are dramatic monologues, but have no other right to be mentioned in this group. *St. Simeon Stylites* is nearer Browning's vein than Tennyson comes elsewhere; it is self-revelation with an irony implied by the poet: one may compare it to the Cardinal ordering his tomb in St. Praxed's. The poem, as I have said above, marks strongly enough Tennyson's dislike to all the extravagances of asceticism: and it stands almost alone among his verses, excepting only the dialect poems, as an instance in which he gave play to that sense of humour which his friends recognized in his talk; for no faculty but humour can perceive at once the pathos and the irony of this spiritual pride which displays itself as an ostentatious humility.

There remains in the group *Lucretius*, which I believe Professor Jebb has rated above all the poet's other work. Full as it is of beauties—beauty of detail and beauty of conception—I cannot rank it among the masterpieces. And yet one might illustrate from it Tennyson's highest qualities; beginning with the superb exposition of Lucretian philosophy, and passing to such lines as these:

> That was mine, my dream, I knew it—
> Of and belonging to me, as the dog
> With *inward yelp and restless forefoot* plies
> His function of the woodland,

where the closeness of observation is matched by

the felicity of phrase; or these, which rival Lucretius in his own stately beauty:

> The Gods, who haunt
> The lucid interspace of world and world,
> Where never creeps a cloud, or moves a wind,
> Nor ever falls the least white star of snow,
> Nor ever lowest roll of thunder moans,
> Nor sound of human sorrow mounts to mar
> Their sacred everlasting calm!

And, better even yet, is the Shakespearean brevity of this:

> Tired of so much within our little life,
> Or of so little in our little life—
> *Poor little life that toddles half an hour*
> *Crown'd with a flower or two, and there an end.*

Yet somehow, as a whole, the poem does not strike its stamp clean and whole upon the mind; and the great passage upon the Gods of Epicurus that I have quoted falls far below the wonderful last stave in the choric chant of *The Lotos-Eaters*.

In *The Lotos-Eaters*, as in *Tithonus*, the inspiration is classical, yet the treatment perfectly individual. The opening description of the sailors coming to the land recalls the manner of Theocritus; but the legend grows in Tennyson's hands. He lifts into a song that longing for repose which is the force within us permanently at war with the aspiration for prolonged activity rendered in *Ulysses*.

> How dull it is to pause, to make an end,
> To rust unburnish'd, not to shine in use!

That is the cry of the world wanderer; and the answering strain to it comes in *The Lotos-Eaters*:

> Why are we weigh'd upon with heaviness,
> And utterly consumed with sharp distress,

While all things else have rest from weariness?
All things have rest: why should we toil alone,
We only toil, who are the first of things,
And make perpetual moan,
Still from one sorrow to another thrown:
Nor ever fold our wings,
And cease from wanderings,
Nor steep our brows in slumber's holy balm;
Nor harken what the inner spirit sings,
"There is no joy but calm!"
Why should we only toil, the roof and crown of things?

I should myself put *Ulysses* and *The Lotos-Eaters* higher than any of the minor poems, except the best of the songs; perhaps above the songs, for, when all is said and done, they are not less beautiful, and they mean more. The theme of *Ulysses* lies in the full course of human thought and endeavour, that of *The Lotos-Eaters* in a back eddy of the stream. For the poem is not a mere fancy; it pictures a tragic forgetfulness. The sense of the world's misery and struggle is present throughout it, though present as a heightening of repose. It was not for nothing that men pictured the gods delighted with the spectacle of human agony:

But they smile, they find a music centred in a doleful song,
Steaming up, a lamentation and an ancient tale of wrong,
Like a tale of little meaning tho' the words are strong.

Men in all ages have made the gods in their own image, and this conception answers to a feeling deeply seated in the human heart, the poignant pleasure of contrast. In the sense of release from action lies half the luxury of repose.

It is strange to compare *The Lotos-Eaters* with a very fine example of Tennyson's later poetry, *The Voyage of Maeldune*. Classical legend is part of the heritage which every scholar receives almost unconsciously; he moulds it to his own temperament, it becomes easily instinct with his own personality. But here Tennyson is fascinated, as any stranger might be, with the Celtic romance, and he writes with extraordinary virtuosity something that keeps the Celtic extravagance, yet restrains it within the discreet bounds of beauty. And the result is absolutely exotic. The fact is worth emphasizing, for many of our poets nowadays run after these new inventions, and seek to find the true sources of inspiration in the legends of a tongue that they have never spoken, and in a literature that has never set its mark on the world. The ways of art are many, but it is as well to point out that Gaelic legend to the educated Scot or Irishman is almost invariably alien, while Greek and Latin stories are in his very blood. Tennyson gave a far more conspicuous proof of this truth when he essayed the story of Arthur. Do what he would, the "matter of Britain" remained intractable, while the older myths that lay about the roots of all modern civilization were freely familiar to his hand.

It is, however, clear that Tennyson's contemporaries clamoured for something more English—though a better expression of the best English spirit than breathes in *Ulysses* cannot be found—and they first took to their hearts the Idyls of English domestic life. The Wordsworthian theory of absolute simplicity still obtained to some degree, and Tennyson records that he found this simplicity the hardest quality to achieve consistently with poetic style. The natural magnificence of his diction had to be laid aside in poems like *Dora*, or the most famous of this group, *Enoch Arden*—though in this last the description of the tropical island gave the chance for a contrast of style—a gorgeous passage set in a narrative otherwise studiously simple. It seems to me that he was turning counter to the bent of his genius in all these efforts; but *Enoch Arden* has been more translated

than any of his poems.   Yet I doubt whether
posterity will greatly care for it.   *The Gardener's
Daughter*, though not of remarkable interest, I
take to be the best of this group; but here there is
no question of simplicity; the style is of a studied
luxuriance, though the sentiment is domestic; the
Gardener's Daughter moves among roses and sunlight.   *Dora* seems to me tame; *Audley Court,
Walking to the Mail*, and *Edwin Morris* are perfectly uninteresting; and *Sea Dreams* is perhaps
the worst thing in the 1842 volume.   All these are
in blank verse, and, I confess, have very little
claim at all, in my opinion, to rank as poetry.
Aylmer's Field is very much better, and the in-
dignant brother's sermon gives Tennyson an opening for that impassioned rhetoric of which he was
so great a master.   His other tales in blank verse:
The Lover's Tale, with its maturer episode of *The
Golden Supper*; *The Sisters* (not the ballad), *The
Ring*, and so forth, are by common consent as near
mediocrity as so excellent an artist could fall.

But among the greatest of these early successes—
greatest that is as successes—were the rhymed idylls
and poems.   *The Miller's Daughter* everyone will
allow to be charming; I cannot allow it to be more.
Lady Clara Vere de Vere and *The Lord of Burleigh*
plainly belong to the epoch of John Leech's ring-
leted young ladies; they are early Victorian with a
vengeance, and to my mind perfectly intolerable.
Worse still is *The May Queen*, which is throughout in a false key of pathos.   Yet these three poems
were perhaps more widely popular than any of his
other work.   They appealed to the public which
now reads *Tit-Bits*.   A later poem, *The Children's
Hospital*, had the good fortune to be less read, but
was very unworthy of its author.   But two others,
The First Quarrel and *The Grandmother*, especially
the latter, rank high among the poet's work.

Still, the bent of Tennyson's mind was not to simplicity. First and last he saw things as he saw them in *The Palace of Art*, with a glow of colour that no man could render better; and when he essayed the poetry of small things, as in *The May Queen*, he was apt to degenerate into a frame of mind that was almost maudlin, and to aim at the cheap and obvious sentiment affected by the ordinary hymn-writer.

Little remains to be classified except the great mass of shorter lyrics. But one may exclude from these three small groups. In one I should class poems like the two *Marianas, The Dream of Fair Women*, and *The Palace of Art*. These are neither lyrics nor narratives; they are for the most part a poetry of sheer pictorial description, masterly in its kind, but by its kind too nearly related to paintings of still life. They have everything that one can desire in poetry except life, and perhaps for that reason lend themselves with exceptional ease to quotation. Quatrain after quatrain may be detached and valued by itself, and this is a sufficient ground for relegating them to a second class in the poet's total achievement.

Not higher than these, but scarcely lower, must be ranked the addresses to the Queen and the royal family. No poet has done this duty of compliment or condolence so well since the days of Horace, largely no doubt for the reason that Tennyson, like Horace, was perfectly sincere in his admiration and gratitude. The laureate never sacrificed the dignity of his art, yet never failed to mark a deep respect which grew into reverence under the sympathy inspired by bereavements which moved the whole nation. With these also might perhaps most fitly be placed such addresses and epistles as are lyrical only in form—though the form is often exquisite. A beautiful example is the invitation to F. D,

Maurice; and the lines to Lord Dufferin are superb;
Horace has nothing to surpass their opening:

> At times our Britain cannot rest,
>   At times her steps are swift and rash,
>   She moving, at her girdle clash
> The golden keys of East and West.
>
> Not swift or rash, when late she lent
>   The sceptre of her West, her East,
>   To one, that ruling has increased
> Her greatness and her self-content.

But indeed the best way to praise Tennyson's
accomplishment in this whole kind of literature,
where grace, dignity, and finish of style are the
first essentials, is to call his work truly Horatian.
Only, when one does so, it should be remembered
that Horace has nothing to show against *Maud* or
The Lotos-Eaters. And I question whether even
Horace has written anything to equal in felicity
the lines *To Virgil*.

I pass to the dialect poems—quite a considerable
group. There are, to begin with, the two *Northern
Farmers*; there is *The Northern Cobbler*, *The Spin-
ster's Sweet-Arts*, *The Village Wife or the Entail*,
Owd Roä, and, in the very last volume, *The Churchwarden and the Curate*. Not one of them but has
something good, some genuine touch of humour:
I quote the last two verses of *The Churchwarden*
(a converted Baptist, who sticks to the Church since
the " Baptises " "weshed their sins in his pond ").

> But Parson 'e *will* speäk out, saw, now 'e be sixty-seven,
> He'll niver swap Owlby an' Scratby fur owt but the Kingdom
>   o' Heaven;
> An' thou'll be 'is Curate 'ere, but, if iver tha meäns to git
>   'igher,
> Tha mun tackle the sins o' the Wo'ld, an' not the faults o' the
>   Squire.

An' I reckons tha'll light of a livin' somewheers i' the Wowd [1]
  or the Fen,
If tha cottons down to thy betters, an' keeäps thysen to thysen.
But niver not speäk plaain out, if tha wants to git forrards a bit,
But creeäp along the hedge-bottoms, an' thou'll be a Bishop yit.

Naay, but tha *mun* speak hout to the Baptises here i' the town,
Fur moäst on 'em talks ageän tithe, an' I'd like tha to preäch
  'em down,
Fur *they*'ve bin a-preächin' *mea* down, they heve, and I haätes
  'em now,
Fur they leäved their nasty sins i' *my* pond, an' it poison'd the
  cow.

Grim enough the humour is at times; the Village
Wife is not an agreeable person; a malicious old
gossip, to put it plain; but the portrait of her
clings very close to the realities of life. *The
Northern Cobbler* is the only spirited thing known
to me that can be read on a teetotal platform, and
Owd Roä is excellent. But the first two—*The
Northern Farmer* (*Old Style*) and *The Northern
Farmer* (*New Style*)—are far beyond the rest. Each
of them sprang, as the *Life* tells us, from a single
sentence. "When I canters my 'erse along the
the ramper (highway), I 'ears proputty, proputty":
there is the germ of *The Northern Farmer* (*New
Style*):

Proputty, proputty's ivrything 'ere, an', Sammy, I'm blest
If it isn't the saäme oop yonder, fur them as 'as it's the best.

Tisn' them as 'as munny as breäks into 'ouses an' steäls,
Them as 'as coäts to their backs an' taäkes their regular meäls.
Noä, but it's them as niver knaws wheer a meäl's to be 'ad.
Taäke my word for it, Sammy, the poor in a loomp is bad.

And if we praise this, what are we to say about the
old-style farmer, whose portrait (Tennyson wrote)
"is founded on the dying words of a farm bailiff,
as reported to me by a great uncle of mine when
verging upon eighty—'God A'mighty little knows

[1] *Wold.*

what He's about a-taking me.   An' Squire will be
so mad an' all '—I conjectured the man from that
one saying"?

This portrait is as living and dramatic as the
other; it is also what the other is not—a poem.
There is essential poetry in the presentment of this
rough old brute (so FitzGerald called him), with his
strong hold on life and his stolid contempt of death.
The whole man and his life are there, crowded into
less than seventy lines, and there also is the unconscious poetry of the life.   This dogged old animal
comes, and after fifty years the waste places rejoice;
they do not blossom like a rose, but they bear fruit
abundantly, and he feels that his life is there:

> Dubbut looök at the waäste: theer warn't not feeäd for a cow;
> Nowt at all but bracken an' fuzz, an' looök at it now—
> Warn't worth nowt a haäcre, an' now theer's lots o' feeäd,
> Fourscoor yows upon it an' some on it down i' seeäd.

That is not just "proputty, proputty"; it is the
pride of a man in his work, perhaps the truest of
all subjects for poetry; and Tennyson makes you
feel the poetry of it behind the half-articulate
utterance.   His old brute does not say:

> I have lived my life, and that which I have done
> May he within himself make pure;

but he does say, I have lived my life and I have
done something; and if I cannot go on living my
own life, I will live no other:

> Git ma my aäle I tell tha, an' if I mun doy I mun doy.

These two poems (but especially the one which
is a poem) must be counted among the elect handful
of Tennyson's work.   You cannot estimate him
fairly without reference to them, for no man working
in verse has excelled them in humorous creative

power since Shakespeare. I would put the man who "stubbed Thornaby waste" beside Ulysses just as confidently as a Rembrandt by a Greek statue. One may regret that this quality of humour was so absent from the larger work of the poet; yet the possession of that faculty must throughout have been a saving grace. *Maud* is extravagant enough and shrill in passages; imagine what it might have been if Tennyson, like his great contemporary, Victor Hugo, had only been endowed with wit. That he kept humour continuously in abeyance and suspense is due, I think, to the inherent classicism of his mind, which aimed above all things at securing a unity of conception and treatment.

Among the lyrics, several easily detach themselves as being properly ballads—that is, lyrical narratives, where the narrative interest preponderates. Such a poem as *The Defence of Lucknow* is little more than a stirring recital of the events of a siege; Lord Roberts, no mean authority, has put on record his admiration for its truth to the facts and feelings of that time. *The Charge of the Light Brigade* is narrative fused into the glow of a war-song, and, hackneyed as the lines are, it is impossible to read them aloud without being caught by the emotion. *The Charge of the Heavy Brigade* is mere narrative; an attempt to repeat a success. But finest of all the ballads is the great poem upon, Sir Richard Grenville and his 'Revenge'. The form, by no means a common one, was almost certainly suggested by Browning's *Hervé Riel*; but *Hervé Riel*, though a spirited poem, has no claim to rank with Tennyson's magnificent work. The inequalities of the metre, which with Browning made a series of roughnesses, are by Tennyson used with the finest effect to mark transitions in the intensity of the narrative; and nothing could exceed the skill with which in the last stave he gives the movement of the storm rising ever higher and higher in attack upon the fleet, till at last there came the final downward plunge and all was lone water, a waste immensity of waves:

> And the little Revenge herself went down by the island crags,
>   To be lost evermore in the main.

This, with *The Charge of the Light Brigade*, probably makes up the only ballad work of Tennyson's which posterity will care about. *Rizpah*, which Mr. Swinburne hailed with a pæan of exaltation as proving decisively Tennyson's superiority to De Musset (in whom Mr. Swinburne saw his French counterpart), is certainly a great poem; yet perhaps too spasmodic in its utterance to be permanently accepted. But in the poems where the passion is more than the events—which are lyrics rather than ballads—he has achieved many minor successes. *The Lady of Shalott* must rank among his best and most characteristic poems. *St. Agnes' Eve* and *Sir Galahad* have a wonderful depth and melody in their very simple versification. Few things in Tennyson are more magical than the opening:

> Deep on the convent-roof the snows
>   Are sparkling to the moon:
> My breath to heaven like vapour goes:
>   May my soul follow soon.

And both of the poems carry one along with a rush and fire that is not found in the later lyrics. *King Cophetua* is another little masterpiece, and so is *The Sailor Boy*.

The greatest of his pure lyrics are to be found, I think, in *Maud* and *In Memoriam*, and with these must be ranked, without a single exception, all the songs in *The Princess*. "Tears, idle tears" is unique in the language. Browning's *One Word*

More and Lamb's delightful lines on the "old familiar faces" are poems, in a sense lyrical, that dispense with rhyme; Collins's *Ode to Evening* has been much praised for the melody of its versification. But none of these is like "Tears, idle tears", which has the absolute movement and quality of song, not less than even such verses as "The splendour falls on castle walls", where everything is done by an elaborate system of single and double rhymes and by repeated refrains to suggest music to the ear. And apart from the haunting charm of the verse, there is poetry of the subtlest kind in this new expression of the thought that Virgil put so inimitably in his

"Sunt lacrimae rerum et mentem mortalia tangunt".

Inimitably, one says, for Tennyson only takes the suggestion; what he has done with it is to make something that baffles translation as effectually as the *lacrimae rerum* itself. Words and thought are blended beyond all possibility of separation; and that is a mark of the very highest poetry. Probably for this reason schoolmasters particularly delight to set hapless boys to torture this passage into Latin elegiacs.

Besides the gems set in caskets of their own there are detached lyrics and to spare in Tennyson's nine hundred pages. Even among the Juvenilia, *The Deserted House* is not easy to forget, and *The Dying Swan* is full of beauty. *Break, break, break*, will always be admirable; so will *Flow down, cold rivulet, to the sea*, and the two lovely stanzas called *Requiescat*:

> Fair is her cottage in its place,
>   Where yon broad water sweetly slowly glides.
> It sees itself from thatch to base
>   Dream in the sliding tides.

> And fairer she, but ah how soon to die!
>   Her quiet dream of life this hour may cease.
> Her peaceful being slowly passes by
>   To some more perfect peace.

It is worth while looking close here to observe the skill with which the studied irregularity of metre is used: the ten-syllable line, introduced in the first stanza to suggest the slow movement of the river, is caught up in the second as if the life were being gradually borne irresistibly out to sea.

The skill of early manhood was, if anything, enhanced in old age, and song stayed with him as long as speech. Very late, indeed, in his work come the exquisite lines on *The Throstle*, mocking the bird's note—

> Summer is coming, summer is coming.
> I know it, I know it, I know it.

And last of all in place, though not absolutely latest in time, is the great lyric, *Crossing the Bar*, which has a thrill in it from the opening words onward that is beyond the power of music to answer —a true inspiration.

A place apart is held by the Funeral Ode on Wellington, which beyond question stands very high indeed among poems written for a fixed occasion. The two opening stanzas are admirable; after them the movement flags somewhat, though with flashes such as this sudden and brilliant transition:—

> Let the bell be toll'd:
> And a deeper knell in the heart be knoll'd;
> And the sound of the sorrowing anthem roll'd
> Thro' the dome of the golden cross;
> And the volleying cannon thunder his loss;
> *He knew their voices of old.*

Then comes the splendid invocation to Nelson, concluding with the refrain—

> With honour, honour, honour, honour to him,
> Eternal honour to his name.

A little farther comes the best-known passage in the whole — that which describes the "path of duty". But finer by far in my judgment is the closing strophe, characteristic alike in thought and in expression, and not so well known but that one may quote it:

> Peace, his triumph will be sung
> By some yet unmoulded tongue
> Far on in summers that we shall not see:
> Peace, it is a day of pain
> For one about whose patriarchal knee
> Late the little children clung:
> O peace, it is a day of pain
> For one, upon whose hand and heart and brain
> Once the weight and fate of Europe hung.
> Ours the pain, be his the gain!
> More than is of man's degree
> Must be with us, watching here
> At this, our great solemnity.
> Whom we see not we revere;
> We revere, and we refrain
> From talk of battles loud and vain,
> And brawling memories all too free
> For such a wise humility
> As befits a solemn fane:
> We revere, and while we hear
> The tides of Music's golden sea
> Setting toward eternity,
> Uplifted high in heart and hope are we,
> Until we doubt not that for one so true
> There must be other nobler work to do
> Than when he fought at Waterloo,
> And Victor he must ever be.
> For tho' the Giant Ages heave the hill
> And break the shore, and evermore
> Make and break, and work their will;
> Tho' world on world in myriad myriads roll
> Round us, each with different powers,
> And other forms of life than ours,

What know we greater than the soul?
On God and Godlike men we build our trust.
Hush! the Dead March wails in the people's ears:
The dark crowd moves, and there are sobs and tears:
The black earth yawns: the mortal disappears;
Ashes to ashes, dust to dust;
He is gone who seem'd so great.—
Gone; but nothing can bereave him
Of the force he made his own
Being here, and we believe him
Something far advanced in State,
And that he wears a truer crown
Than any wreath that man can weave him.
Speak no more of his renown,
Lay your earthly fancies down,
And in the vast cathedral leave him,
God accept him, Christ receive him.

It remains only to point out that in this, as in the very fine stanzas written for the Queen's Jubilee, Tennyson has aimed at a stately rhythm, which followed closely the modulations of prose in their variety and earnestness, yet is lifted into the sphere of poetry by almost imperceptible touches of style. It is this extraordinary command of metre and extraordinary sense of the fitting that stamps Tennyson for the most consummate artist in verse since Keats—and, except Keats, he has no equal till you go back to Milton. His range was of the widest. When he condescended to the merely fanciful, no man ever had a lighter or a prettier touch; witness *The Talking Oak*, *Amphion*, or *Will Waterproof*, a poem which immeasurably goes beyond Praed and Locker in their own peculiar excellences. And in estimating a poet one must always attach some weight to everything that he did well. Few poets in the world have done so many things so well as Tennyson; that does not decide his position, but it constitutes an integral part of his fame.

Chapter VIII.

The Idylls of the King.

My business in this volume is purely with literary criticism, and in this chapter I have simply to estimate and classify the *Idylls* as poetry. There is, however, a formidable literature which has sprung up round the Arthurian story. It is exhaustively treated by Professor Maccallum in his book, *Tennyson's Idylls of the King and Arthurian Legend.* Those who do not care to follow Mr. Maccallum into his recondite researches will find as much as anybody but the special student of mediæval literature requires to know in Professor Saintsbury's volume *The Flourishing of Romance and Rise of Allegory.* Here I need only say that the Arthurian story was one of the three great and fertile subjects for mediæval romance—the matter of France, the matter of Britain, and the matter of Rome. Those tales which centre round Charlemagne are the matter of France; the matter of Rome includes the tale of Troy and the mythical adventures of Alexander of Macedon; the matter of Britain is the Arthuriad in one form or other, and as it was the latest to take definite literary form, so it has lasted longest as an abiding source of inspiration. Professor Maccallum traces it out in all the authors who have treated of it down to the present day, from what one may call its practical inception in the work of Geoffrey of Monmouth. It dates as a completed story from early in the twelfth century; where exactly it came from, the doctors cannot agree to decide. Some say that it was a Welsh or Armorican myth or legend, transmitted to France and there shaped; some that it is devoid of national colour, a mere literary creation;

others, and of these is Professor Saintsbury, that
it was English or Anglo-Norman, at least in its
developed form.   In its crude. state one finds
principally the heroic figure of Arthur, a great
slayer of warriors in the Saxon and Norman wars.
Then gradually comes in the story of Arthur's
fairy origin and his mysterious passing; but only
when the personage of Lancelot and the central
interest of the Holy Grail are blended with the
legend do we find that romance which has inspired
countless poets.   Professor Saintsbury believes
that Walter Map invented Lancelot; at all events,
whoever invented him changed the entire character
of the legend.   Tales of the Saxon and Norman
wars were superseded by the love interest between
Lancelot and Guinevere—the typical invention of
an age in which chivalry, the direct offshoot of
monasticism, despised marriage and saw the romance of love only in passion outside the bond;
and this love interest was heightened by the mystical
quest of the Holy Grail.   Thus upon the story
of passionate but unlawful love was grafted the
extravagant mediæval worship of virginity—again
an offshoot of monasticism; Lancelot, though he
cannot achieve the quest, attempts it, nothing but
his sin of love withstanding him; and what he
cannot win himself is attained by his son, the
maiden knight Galahad.

    We need not inquire here into the different ver-
sions of the legend as told by Chrestien de Troyes
and the rest; for the source of Tennyson's inspiration is clear, the prose romance of Sir Thomas
Malory.   This he supplemented by the Welsh
Mabinogion, translated by Lady Charlotte Guest,
whence he took the Idyll of Enid and Geraint.
But it is important to emphasize at once the character both of Tennyson's work and that of the
sources from which he drew.   Malory's book is

not an epic; it is a romance. The distinction is
so admirably drawn in Professor Ker's *Epic and
Romance* (p. 5) that I make no apology for quotation.

"Whatever Epic may mean, it implies some weight
and solidity; Romance means nothing, if it does not
convey some notion of mystery and fantasy. . . . The
two great kinds of narrative literature in the Middle
Ages might be distinguished by their favourite incidents
and commonplaces of adventure. No kind of adventure
is so common or better told in the earlier heroic manner
than the defence of a narrow place against odds. Such
are the stories of Hamther and Sorli in the hall of
Ermanaric, of the Niblung kings in the hall of Attila, of
the Fight of Finnesburh, of Walter at the Wasgestein,
of Byrhtnoth at Maldon, of Roland in the Pyrenees"
[and, I may add, of Ulysses in the hall at Ithaca against
the suitors]. "The favourite adventure of mediæval
romance is something different—a knight riding alone
through a forest; another knight; a shock of lances;
a fight on foot with swords, ' racing, tracing, and foin-
ing like two wild boars'; then, perhaps, recognition—
the two knights belong to the same household and are
engaged in the same quest. This collision of blind
forces, this tournament at random, takes the place, in
the French romances, of the older kind of combat. In
the older kind the parties have always good reasons of
their own for fighting; they do not go into it with the
same sort of readiness as the wandering champions of
romance."

There is nothing fantastic about the epic; it is
practically a drama narrated, as Aristotle saw; it is
of the stuff of life.

"If its characters are not men, they are nothing; not
even thoughts or allegories; they cannot go on talking
unless they have something to do; and so the whole
stuff of life comes boldly into the epic poem."[1]

[1] Ker, *Epic and Romance*, p. 10.

Romance, on the other hand, depends upon a picturesque condition of the external environment; Ulysses may ride in a cart, Lancelot cannot without sore disgrace. And consequently, because romance shuts its eyes to the trivial, its scenes naturally are conceived with "the more airy mode of imagination". Tennyson has felt strongly the need of this, and his actors move among wonderful blue landscapes, or by lonely meres; they dwell in houses, it is true, but their dwelling is in "the dim rich city" Camelot, built like a dream, and like a dream to vanish. He is committed to romance because his aim is allegorical; for if in your allegory the characters assume real flesh and blood, what abstraction can compete with that interest?

To a certain extent the *Idylls of the King*, in so far as they relate the life and passing of Arthur, are comparable with such an artificial epic as Virgil's *Æneid*. Like the *Æneid*, they tell a story taken out of books, not direct from life itself; they are a work of the literary imagination; and this is what Tennyson meant, no doubt, when he wrote, in the sort of prelude to the *Morte d'Arthur*, of an "epic" that had been attempted and burnt—

His epic, his King Arthur in twelve books.

Like Virgil, he is choosing a picturesque subject out of the nation's half-mythical past; like Virgil, he is professedly describing the temper and the doings of a time divided from him by dead faiths and forgotten centuries; like Virgil, he relies chiefly upon the literary beauty of his workmanship. But, unlike Virgil, he abandons the direct continuity of narrative which is the formal characteristic of the literary epic; and, unlike Virgil's, his purpose is confessedly allegorical.

Too much can easily be made of the allegorical

aspect. Tennyson got interested in the stories he
retold, as was inevitable: and in proportion as he
grew interested the allegory tended to disappear.
In the earlier-written Idylls, allegory there is
little or none. *Vivien* certainly indicates the moral
purpose, but the story is told for its own sake:
Enid, Gareth and Lynette, and *Elaine* are simply
tales taken direct from the *Mabinogion* and Malory
and beautifully retold; *Guinevere* insists again upon
the moral purpose, but beyond that is in no way
allegorical that I can see. It is when we come to
the Idylls written later to complete the cycle, *The
Coming of Arthur*, *The Holy Grail*, and *The Last
Tournament*, that we feel ourselves distracted between what is said and what implied. Here the
narrative is less, and the beauty of detached passages more; and in the final canto, *The Passing
of Arthur*, there is added to the original *Morte
d'Arthur* not only a prologue describing Arthur's
moods and doubts before the "last great battle in
the West", but also some thirty lines of epilogue
which emphasize the religious or metaphysical symbolism of the legend. What that symbolism, as
distinct from the obvious moral purpose, precisely
implies I do not know, nor do I care to fix a meaning; Tennyson himself deprecated a too exact interpretation, and one may read, as I have said,
several of the *Idylls* without temptation to seek it,
and all without the need to go beyond the surface
beauty of the narrative. But of the intention there is
no doubt, and no doubt also that it was there from
the first. Indeed, we have been spared much. In
the *Life*, Lord Tennyson gives a first draft sketched
about 1833, in which the two Guineveres of the
original story were to figure, one representing
primitive Christianity, the other Roman Catholi-
cism, while the Round Table stood for Liberal
Institutions, and King Arthur himself typified

religious Faith. Yet at the same time Tennyson was writing *The Lady of Shalott, St. Agnes' Eve*, and *Sir Galahad*, which are all in the key of pure lyrical romance, and show the full fascination of the legend itself. He was too good a poet to become a slave to an allegory, but, for all that, in his moral ardour he twisted the whole story clean out of its original shape; and unfortunately the shape was essential to the spirit. The tale of Troy, as Homer told it, has made the stuff of poetry for all ages; it deals with simple and universal human motives, the solid business of life. But the legend of Arthur and his knights, as we read it in Malory or elsewhere, is a legend of knight-errantry, involving the whole creed of chivalry. Now, chivalry is the direct offspring of monasticism; of that mediæval conception of faith by which the highest ideal of life lay in virginity; and your warrior knight, finding that the world could not get on without love between the sexes, compromised for his ideal by a sort of super-sensual love-making. Marriage was looked upon as a concession to our gross nature; heroic love aimed at nothing beyond free service and worship to the woman of the heart's choice. The love of any husband for his wife could not fulfil the conditions of the ideal; the love of Lancelot for Guinevere was ideal save in so far as it lowered itself to earthly passion; and but for this sin Lancelot would have achieved the quest of the Grail, which Arthur never essayed. It is permitted to Lancelot to achieve it, not indeed in his own person, but through his son, Galahad, the maiden knight. Thus the story holds together, and centres round Lancelot and Galahad, who is Lancelot glorified. It is essentially a literature of that science of love, which knights, ladies, and minstrels discussed and elaborated in the courts of Provence.

Tennyson takes this whole cycle of stories, and

makes them into an allegory, which for its plainest lesson inculcates the various moral effects of love; and instantly the new wine bursts the old bottles. His highest ideal is love in marriage; "to love one woman only and to cleave to her"; man's highest profession is that of Arthur to Guinevere: "For I was ever virgin save for thee". Arthur with him is the centre of the story: or rather the story has two centres, for Galahad still achieves the Grail; and Tennyson can only reconcile the two ideals by representing Galahad's choice, if fit at all, as fit only for exceptional sanctities of nature. Thus he departs from the good faith of the legend, and shows us knight-errantry, always hard to believe in, still more incredible because stripped of its real inspiration.

The change of focus has of course necessitated many changes in the story. In the *Morte d'Arthur*, written twenty years before the other Idylls, Tennyson held very close indeed to Malory; except for Arthur's speech, of the "old order changeth, yielding place to new", there is little hint of the framework which was to come. But in 1858 he went back to the cycle, and first took in hand the tale of Vivien. Vivien or Nimue in Malory is simply a damsel whom Merlin persecutes with importunity, and who, by a woman's wit, contrives to shut him within a prison of his own devising. In Tennyson she is the seed of a corruption which spreads through the court; a seed of Mark's sowing, for he sends his paramour deliberately to break up the triumphant honesty of Arthur's knightly companionship. Into *Enid* is introduced a moral strangely at variance with the ideas of chivalry; for Arthur contrasts the moral victory over himself won by Edyrn with Geraint's exploits, and censures the prince for his wild adventure, which Malory would surely have applauded. Gawain also in the old legends is one of the greatest and most courteous knights; yet his treachery to Sir Pelleas may be held to give Tennyson some ground for treating him as the example of fickleness in love; a tilter and fighter destitute of the nobler qualities of heart. But the retribution which Malory does concern himself to exact is not from the faithless Gawain but from the cruel Ettarre; cruelty is a worse crime than faithlessness to his eyes; and so Nimue, the damsel of the Lake, throws a charm upon Ettarre, by which she must love Pelleas and he be cold to her, so that at the last Ettarre dies from love-sickness. Likewise Tristram and "la beale Isoude" are in no way accounted pernicious examples, but rather held up for imitation as the perfect union of valiant knight and fair lady, coupled continually with the fame of Lancelot and Guinevere; and the erring queen with her supreme knight is the centre and soul of the whole legend. Lancelot is the queen's protector. When Guinevere is accused of poisoning a knight at her table, she has no recourse but to Lancelot's kinsmen to find a champion, since he himself has left the kingdom at her bidding, given in a moment of jealous anger; Arthur must stand by and see, and if no champion be forthcoming, or if the champion be worsted, then he must order his queen to the stake. But Sir Bors sends hasty messengers to Lancelot, and at the last moment, when Bors is already in the lists, Lancelot rides in to take his place and overthrow the challenger, Sir Mador de la Port. Arthur bulks largely in the opening of the book; but as the story develops and the love interest heightens, Lancelot grows more and more the central figure, and the tale, as Malory tells it, closes, not with the passing of Arthur, but with the death of Lancelot, who from being knight-errant passes into the convent, not thwarting, but fulfilling,

the whole tenor of his life.   Yet he was buried not
as monk, but as prince in his own chapel at Joyous
Gard, where came Sir Ector de Maris, his brother,
and heard singing and praying and saw lights in
the choir.

"Then went Sir Bors unto Sir Ector and told him
how there lay his brother, Sir Launcelot, dead.   And
then Sir Ector threw his shield, sword, and helm from
him; and when he beheld Sir Launcelot's visage, he
fell down in a swoon; and when he awaked, it were
hard for any tongue to tell the doleful complaints that
he made for his brother. 'Ah, Launcelot,' said he,
'thou wert head of all Christian knights.'   'And now,
I dare say,' said Sir Bors, 'thou Sir Launcelot, there
thou liest, that thou wert never matched of earthly
knight's hands; and thou wert the courtliest knight that
ever bare shield; and thou wert the truest friend to thy
lover that ever bestrode horse; and thou wert the truest
lover of a sinful man that ever loved woman; and thou
wert the kindest man that ever strake with sword; and
thou wert the goodliest person that ever came among
press of knights; and thou wert the meekest man, and
the gentlest, that ever ate in hall among ladies; and
thou wert the sternest knight to thy mortal foe that
ever put spear in the rest.' "

There, as I say, you have the true inspiration of
the legend.   Lancelot was a sinner, but a sinner
who came nearer to salvation than King Arthur
treading the beaten highway of marriage, sitting
at home a governor, not riding errant for adventure.
Such was the view of those who shaped the legend,
and who saw in this world nothing of much consequence for itself, but a pathway to hell or Paradise.   For a man to take and handle the tale as
Tennyson has handled it, is as though he should
rewrite the *Iliad* from the standpoint of the Atridæ,
to bring out the evil consequences of insubordina-

tion. Malory no more blames Lancelot for his love
than Homer censures Achilles for his wrath.

A comparison with Malory thus makes one feel,
as I think, the ineradicable vice of Tennyson's
scheme.   But not less certainly it brings into relief
the fineness of his art; and since few except professed students read the old knight, it seems worth
while to print here in full the story of Elaine as he
tells it; there is no other way so good for showing
what Tennyson took in suggestion, and what he
added in form and detail.

" Within a fifteen days of that feast the king let cry a
great justs and a tournament that should be at that day
at Camelot, that is Winchester.   And the king let cry
that he and the king of Scots would just against all
that would come against them.   And when this cry was
made, thither came many knights.   So there came
thither the king of Northgalis, and king Anguish of
Ireland, and the king with the hundred knights, and Sir
Galahalt the haut prince, and the king of Northumberland, and many other noble dukes and earls of divers
countries.   So king Arthur made him ready to depart
to these justs, and would have had the queen with him :
but at that time she would not, she said, for she was
sick and might not ride at that time.   That me repenteth, said the king, for this seven year ye saw not
such a fellowship together, except at Whitsuntide when
Galahad departed from the court.   Truly, said the queen
to the king, ye must hold me excused, I may not be
there, and that me repenteth.   And many deemed the
queen would not be there because of Sir Launcelot du
Lake, for Sir Launcelot would not ride with the king ;
for he said he was not whole of the wound the which Sir
Mador had given him.   Wherefore the king was heavy
and passing wroth, and so he departed towards Winchester with his fellowship.   And so by the way the
king lodged in a town called Astolat, that is now in
English called Gilford, and there the king lay in the
castle.   So when the king was departed, the queen

called Sir Launcelot unto her, and said, Sir Launcelot ye are greatly to blame, thus to hold you behind my lord: what trow ye, what will your enemies and mine say and deem? nought else but see how Sir Launcelot holdeth him ever behind the king, and so doth the queen, for that they would be together; and thus will they say, said the queen to Sir Launcelot, have ye no doubt thereof.

" Madam, said Sir Launcelot, I allow your wit, it is of late come sin ye were wise, and therefore, madam, as at this time I will be ruled by your counsel, and this night I will take my rest, and to-morrow by time will take my way toward Winchester. But wit you well, said Sir Launcelot to the queen, that at the justs I will be against the king and all his fellowship. Ye may there do as ye list, said the queen, but by my counsel ye shall not be against your king and your fellowship, for therein be full many hardy knights of your blood, as ye wot well enough, it needeth not to rehearse them. Madam, said Sir Launcelot, I pray you that ye be not displeased with me, for I will take the adventure that God will send me. And so upon the morn early Sir Launcelot heard mass, and brake his fast, and so took his leave of the queen, and departed. And then he rode so much until he came to Astolat, that is Gilford; and there it happed him in the eventide he came to an old baron's place, that hight Sir Bernard of Astolat. And as Sir Launcelot entered into his lodging, king Arthur espied him as he did walk in a garden beside the castle, how he took his lodging, and knew him full well. It is well, said king Arthur unto the knights that were with him in that garden beside the castle, I have now espied one knight that will play his play at the justs to the which we be gone toward, I undertake he will do marvels. Who is that, we pray you tell us, said many knights that were there at that time. Ye shall not wit for me, said the king, at this time. And so the king smiled, and went to his lodging. So when Sir Launcelot was in his lodging, and unarmed him in his chamber, the old baron and hermit came unto him, making his reverence, and welcomed him in

the best manner; but the old knight knew not Sir
Launcelot. Fair sir, said Sir Launcelot to his host, I
would pray you to lend me a shield that were not
openly known, for mine is well known. Sir, said his
host, ye shall have your desire, for me seemeth ye be
one of the likeliest knights of the world, and therefore I
shall shew you friendship. Sir, wit you well I have two
sons which were but late made knights, and the eldest
hight Sir Tirre, and he was hurt that same day that he
was made knight, that he may not ride, and his shield
ye shall have, for that is not known, I dare say, but
here and in no place else. And my youngest son hight
Sir Lavaine, and if it please you he shall ride with you
unto that justs, and he is of his age strong and wight.
For much my heart giveth unto you that ye should be a
noble knight, therefore, I pray you tell me your name,
said Sir Bernard. As for that, said Sir Launcelot, ye
must hold me excused as at this time, and if God give
me grace to speed well at the justs I shall come again
and tell you. But I pray you, said Sir Launcelot, in
any wise let me have your son Sir Lavaine with me,
and that I may have his brother's shield. Also this
shall be done, said Sir Bernard.

"The old baron had a daughter that time that was
called that time the fair maid of Astolat. And ever she
beheld Sir Launcelot wonderfully. And, as the book
saith, she cast such a love unto Sir Launcelot that she
could never withdraw her love, wherefore she died; and
her name was Elaine le Blank. So thus as she came to
and fro, she was so hot in her love that she besought
Sir Launcelot to wear upon him at the justs a token of
hers. Fair damsel, said Sir Launcelot, and if I grant
you that, ye may say I do more for your love than ever
I did for lady or damsel. Then he remembered him
that he would go to the justs disguised, and for because
he had never afore that time borne no manner of token
of no damsel, then he bethought him that he would bear
one of her, that none of his blood thereby might know
him. And then he said, Fair maiden, I will grant you
to wear a token of yours upon my helmet, and therefore what it is show it me. Sir, she said, it is a red

sleeve of mine, of scarlet well embroidered with great pearls. And so she brought it him. So Sir Launcelot received it and said, Never did I erst so much for no damsel. And then Sir Launcelot betook the fair maiden his shield in keeping, and prayed her to keep that until that he came again. And so that night he had merry rest and great cheer. For ever the damsel Elaine was about Sir Launcelot, all the while she might be suffered.

"So upon a day on the morn, king Arthur and all his knights departed; for their king had tarried there three days to abide his noble knights. And so when the king was riden, Sir Launcelot and Sir Lavaine made them ready for to ride, and either of them had white shields, and the red sleeve Sir Launcelot let carry with him. And so they took their leave at Sir Bernard the old baron, and at his daughter the fair maiden of Astolat. And then they rode so long till they came to Camelot, that time called Winchester. And there was great press of kings, dukes, earls, and barons, and many noble knights. But there Sir Launcelot was lodged privily, by the means of Sir Lavaine, with a rich burgess, that no man in that town was ware what they were. And so they sojourned there till our Lady Day, Assumption, as the great feast should be. So then trumpets blew unto the field, and king Arthur was set on high upon a scaffold, to behold who did best. But, as the French book saith, king Arthur would not suffer Sir Gawaine to go from him, for never had Sir Gawaine the better an Sir Launcelot were in the field; and many times was Sir Gawaine rebuked when Launcelot came into any justs disguised. Then some of the kings, as king Anguish of Ireland and the king of Scotland, were that time turned upon the side of king Arthur. And then on the other party was the king of Northgalis, and the king with the hundred knights, and the king of Northumberland, and Sir Galahalt the haut prince. But these three kings and this duke were passing weak to hold against king Arthur's party: for with him were the noblest knights of the world. So then they withdrew them either party from other, and every man made him

ready in his best manner to do what he might.   Then
Sir Launcelot made him ready, and put the red sleeve
upon his head, and fastened it fast; and so Sir Launcelot and Sir Lavaine departed out of Winchester privily,
and rode until a little leaved wood, behind the party
that held against king Arthur's party, and there they
held them still till the parties smote together.   And
then came in the king of Scots and the king of Ireland
on Arthur's party: and against them came the king of
Northumberland; and the king with the hundred knights
smote down the king of Northumberland, and the king
with the hundred knights smote down king Anguish of
Ireland.   Then Sir Palamides, that was on Arthur's
party, encountered with Sir Galahalt, and either of them
smote down other, and either party halp their lords on
horseback again.   So there began a strong assail upon
both parties.   And then there came in Sir Brandiles,
Sir Sagramor le Desirous, Sir Dodinas le Savage, Sir
Kay le Seneschal, Sir Griflet le Fise de Dieu, Sir
Mordred, Sir Meliot de Logris, Sir Ozanna le Cure
Hardy, Sir Safere, Sir Epinogris, and Sir Galleron of
Galway.   All these fifteen knights were knights of the
Table Round.   So these with more others came in
together, and beat on back the king of Northumberland,
and the king of North Wales. ' When Sir Launcelot
saw this, as he hoved in a little leaved wood, then
he said unto Sir Lavaine, See yonder is a company of
good knights, and they hold them together as boars
that were chafed with dogs.   That is truth, said Sir
Lavaine.

"Now, said Sir Launcelot, an ye will help me a
little, ye shall see yonder fellowship which chaseth now
these men in our side, that they shall go as fast backward as they went forward.   Sir, spare not, said Sir
Lavaine, for I shall do what I may.   Then Sir Launcelot and Sir Lavaine came in at the thickest of the press,
and there Sir Launcelot smote down Sir Brandiles, Sir
Sagramor, Sir Dodinas, Sir Kay, Sir Griflet, and all this
he did with one spear.   And Sir Lavaine smote down
Sir Lucan le Buttelere, and Sir Bedivere.   And then Sir
Launcelot gat another spear, and there he smote down

Sir Agravaine, Sir Gaheris, and Sir Mordred, and Sir
Meliot de Logris. And Sir Lavaine smote down Ozanna
le Cure Hardy: and then Sir Launcelot drew his sword,
and there he smote on the right hand and on the left
hand, and by great force he unhorsed Sir Safere, Sir
Epinogris, and Sir Galleron. And then the knights of
the Table Round withdrew them aback, after they had
gotten their horses as well as they might. O mercy,
said Sir Gawaine, what knight is yonder, that doth so
marvellous deeds of arms in that field? I wot what he
is, said king Arthur. But as at this time I will not
name him. Sir, said Sir Gawaine, I would say it were
Sir Launcelot, by his riding and his buffets that I see
him deal: but ever me seemeth it should not be he, for
that he beareth the red sleeve upon his head, for I wist
him never bear token, at no justs, of lady nor gentlewoman. Let him be, said king Arthur, he will be better
known and do more or ever he depart. Then the party
that were against king Arthur were well comforted, and
then they held them together, that beforehand were sore
rebuked. Then Sir Bors, Sir Ector de Maris, and Sir
Lionel, called unto them the knights of their blood, as
Sir Blamor de Ganis, Sir Bleoberis, Sir Aliduke, Sir
Galihud, Sir Galihodin, Sir Bellangere le Beuse, so
these nine knights of Sir Launcelot's kin thrust in
mightily, for they were all noble knights. And they,
of great hate and despite that they had unto him,
thought to rebuke that noble knight Sir Launcelot, and
Sir Lavaine, for they knew them not. And so they
came hurtling together, and smote down many knights
of Northgalis and of Northumberland. And when Sir
Launcelot saw them fare so, he gat a spear in his hand,
and there encountered with him all at once Sir Bors, Sir
Ector, and Sir Lionel, and all they three smote him at
once with their spears. And with force of themselves
they smote Sir Launcelot's horse to the earth. And by
misfortune Sir Bors smote Sir Launcelot through the
shield into the side, and the spear brake, and the head
left still in his side. When Sir Lavaine saw his master
lie on the ground, he ran to the king of Scots, and
smote him to the earth, and by great force he took his

horse and brought him to Sir Launcelot, and maugre
them all he made him to mount upon that horse.   And
then Launcelot gat a spear in his hand, and there he
smote Sir Bors horse and man to the earth, in the same
wise he served Sir Ector and Sir Lionel, and Sir Lavaine
smote down Sir Blamor de Ganis.   And then Sir Launcelot drew his sword, for he felt himself so sore and hurt
that he wend there to have had his death.   And then he
smote Sir Bleoberis such a buffet on the helmet that he
fell down to the earth in a swoon.   And in the same
wise he served Sir Aliduke and Sir Galihud.   And Sir
Lavaine smote down Sir Bellangere, that was the son
of Alisander le Orphelin.   And by this was Sir Bors
horsed, and then he came with Sir Ector and Sir Lionel,
and all they three smote with swords upon Sir Launcelot's helmet.   And when he felt their buffets, and his
wound the which was so grievous, then he thought to
do what he might while he might endure; and then he
gave Sir Bors such a buffet that he made him bow his
head passing low, and therewithal he rased off his helm,
and might have slain him, and so pulled him down.
And in the same wise he served Sir Ector and Sir Lionel.
For, as the book saith, he might have slain them, but
when he saw their visages his heart might not serve him
thereto, but left them there.

" And then afterward he hurled in the thickest press
of them all, and did there the marvellousest deeds of
arms that ever man saw or heard speak of; and ever Sir
Lavaine the good knight with him.   And there Sir
Launcelot with his sword smote and pulled down, as
the French book maketh mention, more than thirty
knights, and the most party were of the Table Round.
And Sir Lavaine did full well that day, for he smote
down ten knights of the Table Round.

" Mercy, said Sir Gawaine to Arthur, I marvel what
knight that he is with the red sleeve.   Sir, said king
Arthur, he will be known or he depart.   And then the
king blew unto lodging, and the prize was given by
heralds unto the knight with the white shield, that
bare the red sleeve.   Then came the king with the
hundred knights, the king of Northgalis, and the king

of Northumberland, and Sir Galahalt the haut prince, and said unto Sir Launcelot, Fair knight, God thee bless, for much have ye done this day for us, therefore we pray you that ye will come with us, that ye may receive the honour and the prize as ye have worshipfully deserved it. My fair lords, said Sir Launcelot, wit you well, if I have deserved thank I have sore bought it, and that me repenteth, for I am like never to escape with my life, therefore, fair lords, I pray you that ye will suffer me to depart where me liketh, for I am sore hurt. I take none force of none honour, for I had lever to repose me than to be lord of all the world. And therewithal he groaned piteously, and rode a great gallop away-ward from them, until he came under a wood's side; and when he saw that he was from the field nigh a mile, that he was sure that he might not be seen, then he said with an high voice, O gentle knight Sir Lavaine, help me that this truncheon were out of my side, for it sticketh so sore that it nigh slayeth me. O mine own lord, said Sir Lavaine, I would fain do that might please you, but I dread me sore, and I draw out the truncheon, that ye shall be in peril of death. I charge you, said Sir Launcelot, as ye love me draw it out. And therewithal he descended from his horse, and right so did Sir Lavaine, and forthwith Sir Lavaine drew the truncheon out of his side. And he gave a great shriek, and a marvellous grisly groan, and his blood brast out nigh a pint at once, and at last he sank down, and so swooned pale and deadly. Alas, said Sir Lavaine, what shall I do? And then he turned Sir Launcelot into the wind, but so he lay there nigh half an hour as he had been dead. And so at the last Sir Launcelot cast up his eyes, and said, O Lavaine, help me that I were on my horse, for here is fast by within this two mile a gentle hermit, that sometime was a full noble knight and a great lord of possessions: and for great goodness he hath taken him to wilful poverty, and forsaken many lands, and his name is Sir Baudewin of Brittany, and he is a full noble surgeon, and a good leech. Now let see, help me up that I were there. For ever my heart giveth me that I shall never die of my cousin-german's

hands. And then with great pain Sir Lavaine halp him
upon his horse; and then they rode a great gallop
together, and ever Sir Launcelot bled that it ran down
to the earth. And so by fortune they came to that
hermitage, which was under a wood, and a great cliff
on the other side, and a fair water running under it.
And then Sir Lavaine beat on the gate with the butt of
his spear, and cried fast, Let in for Jesu's sake. And
there came a fair child to them, and asked them what
they would? Fair son, said Sir Lavaine, go and pray
thy lord the hermit for God's sake to let in here a knight
that is full sore wounded, and this day tell thy lord that
I saw him do more deeds of arms than ever I heard say
that any man did. So the child went in lightly, and
then he brought the hermit, the which was a passing
good man. So when Sir Lavaine saw him, he prayed
him for God's sake of succour. What knight is he?
said the hermit, is he of the house of king Arthur or
not? I wot not, said Sir Lavaine, what is he, nor what
is his name, but well I wot I saw him do marvellously
this day, as of deeds of arms. On whose party was he?
said the hermit. Sir, said Sir Lavaine, he was this day
against king Arthur, and there he wan the prize of all
the knights of the Round Table. I have seen the day,
said the hermit, I would have loved him the worse
because he was against my lord, king Arthur, for
sometime I was one of the fellowship of the Round
Table, but I thank God now I am otherwise disposed.
But where is he? let me see him. Then Sir Lavaine
brought the hermit to him.

   " And when the hermit beheld him as he sat leaning
upon his saddle-bow, ever bleeding piteously, and ever the
knight hermit thought that he should know him, but he
could not bring him to knowledge, because he was so
pale for bleeding, What knight are ye? said the hermit,
and where were ye born? My fair lord, said Sir Launcelot, I am a stranger, and a knight adventurous that
laboureth throughout many realms for to win worship.
Then the hermit advised him better, and saw by a
wound on his cheek that he was Sir Launcelot. Alas,
said the hermit, mine own lord, why hide you your name

from me: forsooth, I ought to know you of right, for
ye are the most noblest knight of the world; for well I
know you for Sir Launcelot. Sir, said he, sith ye know
me, help me and ye may, for God's sake; for I would
be out of this pain at once, either to death or to life.
Have ye no doubt, said the hermit, ye shall live and fare
right well. And so the hermit called to him two of his
servants, and so he and his servants bare him into the
hermitage, and lightly unarmed him and laid him in his
bed. And then anon the hermit stanchèd his blood,
and made him to drink good wine, so that Sir Launcelot
was well refreshed, and knew himself. For in those
days it was not the guise of hermits as is nowadays.
For there were none hermits in those days but that they
had been men of worship and of prowess, and those
hermits held great household, and refreshed people that
were in distress.

"Now turn we unto king Arthur, and leave we Sir
Launcelot in the hermitage. So when the kings were
come together on both parties, and the great feast
should be holden, king Arthur asked the king of
Northgalis and their fellowship where was that knight
that bare the red sleeve:—Bring him before me, that he
may have his laud and honour and the prize, as it is
right. Then spake Sir Galahalt the haut prince, and
the king with the hundred knights: We suppose that
knight is mischieved, and that he is never like to see
you, nor none of us all, and that is the greatest pity
that ever we wist of any knight. Alas, said Arthur,
how may this be? Is he so hurt? What is his name?
said king Arthur. Truly, said they all, we know not
his name, nor from whence he came, nor whither he
would. Alas, said the king, these be to me the worst
tidings that came to me this seven year: for I would not
for all the lands I hold, to know and wit it were so that
that noble knight were slain. Know ye him? said they
all. As for that, said Arthur, whether I know him or
know him not, ye shall not know for me what man he
is, but Almighty Jesu send me good tidings of him.
And so said they all. By my head, said Sir Gawaine, if
it be so, that the good knight be so sore hurt, it is

great damage and pity to all this land, for he is one of
the noblest knights that ever I saw in a field handle a
spear or a sword. And if he may be found I shall find
him, for I am sure he is not far from this town. Bear
you well, said king Arthur, and ye may find him, unless
that he be in such a plight that he may not hold himself.
Jesu defend, said Sir Gawaine, but wit I shall what he
is, and I may find him. Right so, Sir Gawaine took a
squire with him, upon hackneys, and rode all about
Camelot within six or seven miles. But so he came
again, and could hear no word of him.

"Then within two days king Arthur and all the fellowship returned unto London again. And so as they rode
by the way, it happed Sir Gawaine at Astolat to lodge
with Sir Bernard, there as was Sir Launcelot lodged.
And so as Sir Gawaine was in his chamber to repose
him, Sir Bernard the old baron came unto him, and
his daughter Elaine, for to cheer him, and to ask him
what tidings, and who did best at that tournament of
Winchester. Truly, said Sir Gawaine, there were two
knights that bare two white shields; but the one of
them bare a red sleeve upon his head, and certainly he
was one of the best knights that ever I saw just in field.
For I dare say, said Sir Gawaine, that one knight with
the red sleeve smote down forty valiant knights of the
Table Round, and his fellow did right well and worshipfully. Now blessed be God, said the fair maiden of
Astolat, that that knight sped so well, for he is the man
in the world that I first loved, and truly he shall be the
last that ever I shall love. Now, fair maid, said Sir
Gawaine, is that good knight your love? Certainly, sir,
said she, wit ye well he is my love. Then know ye his
name? said Sir Gawaine. Nay, truly, said the damsel,
I know not his name nor from whence he cometh, but
to say that I love him, I promise you and God that I
love him. How had ye knowledge of him first? said
Sir Gawaine.

"Then she told him as ye have heard tofore, and how
her father betook him her brother to do him service,
and how her father lent him her brother Sir Tirre's
shield,—And here with me he left his own shield. For

what cause did he so? said Sir Gawaine. For this cause, said the damsel, for his shield was too well known among many noble knights. Ah, fair damsel, said Sir Gawaine, please if you let me have a sight of that shield. Sir, said she, it is in my chamber covered with a case, and if ye will come with me, ye shall see it. Not so, said Sir Bernard, till his daughter let send for it. So when the shield was come, Sir Gawaine took off the case: and when he beheld that shield, he knew anon that it was Sir Launcelot's shield, and his own arms. Ah, mercy, said Sir Gawaine, now is my heart more heavier then ever it was tofore. Why? said Elaine. For I have great cause, said Sir Gawaine: is that knight that owneth this shield your love? Yea truly, said she, my love he is, God would I were his love. Truly, said Sir Gawaine, fair damsel, ye have right, for, an he be your love, ye love the most honourable knight of the world, and the man of most worship. So me thought ever, said the damsel, for never, or that time, for no knight that ever I saw loved I never none erst. God grant, said Sir Gawaine, that either of you may rejoice other, but that is in a great adventure. But truly, said Sir Gawaine unto the damsel, ye may say ye have a fair grace, for why, I have known that noble knight this four and twenty year, and never or that day I nor none other knight, I dare make it good, saw nor heard say that ever he bare token or sign of no lady, gentle- woman, nor maiden, at no justs nor tournament. And therefore, fair maiden, said Sir Gawaine, ye are much beholden to him to give him thanks. But I dread me, said Sir Gawaine, that ye shall never see him in this world, and that is great pity that ever was of earthly knight. Alas, said she, how may this be? Is he slain? I say not so, said Sir Gawaine, but wit ye well, he is grievously wounded, by all manner of signs, and by men's sight more likely to be dead then to be on live; and wit ye well he is the noble knight Sir Launcelot, for by this shield I know him. Alas, said the fair maiden of Astolat, how may this be, and what was his hurt? Truly, said Sir Gawaine, the man in the world that loved him best hurt him so, and I dare say, said

Sir Gawaine, an that knight that hurt him knew the
very certainty that he had hurt Sir Launcelot, it would
be the most sorrow that ever came to his heart.   Now,
fair father, said then Elaine, I require you give me
leave to ride and to seek him, or else I wot well I shall
go out of my mind, for I shall never stint till that I find
him and my brother Sir Lavaine.   Do as it liketh you,
said her father, for me right sore repenteth of the hurt
of that noble knight.   Right so the maid made her
ready, and before Sir Gawaine making great dole.
Then on the morn Sir Gawaine came to king Arthur,
and told him how he had found Sir Launcelot's shield
in the keeping of the fair maiden of Astolat.   All that
knew I aforehand, said king Arthur, and that caused me
I would not suffer you to have ado at the great justs:
for I espied, said King Arthur, when he came in till his
lodging, full late in the evening in Astolat.   But marvel
have I, said Arthur, that ever he would bear any sign
of any damsel: for, or now, I never heard say nor knew
that ever he bare any token of none earthly woman.
By my head, said Sir Gawaine, the fair maiden of
Astolat loveth him marvellously well; what it meaneth
I cannot say; and is ridden after to seek him.   So the
king and all came to London, and there Sir Gawaine
openly disclosed to all the court that it was Sir Launcelot that justed best.

"And when Sir Bors heard that, wit ye well he was
a heavy man, and so were all his kinsmen.   But when
queen Guenever wist that Sir Launcelot bare the red
sleeve of the fair maiden of Astolat, she was nigh out
of her mind for wrath.   And then she sent for Sir Bors
de Ganis in all the haste that might be.   So when Sir
Bors was come tofore the queen, then she said, Ah, Sir
Bors, have ye heard say how falsely Sir Launcelot hath
betrayed me?   Alas, madam, said Sir Bors, I am afraid
he hath betrayed himself, and us all.   No force, said
the queen, though he be destroyed, for he is a false
traitor knight.   Madam, said Sir Bors, I pray you say
ye not so, for wit you well I may not hear such language of him.   Why, Sir Bors, said she, should I not
call him traitor, when he bare the red sleeve upon his

head at Winchester, at the great justs? Madam, said Sir Bors, that sleeve-bearing repenteth me sore, but I dare say he did it to none evil intent, but for this cause he bare the red sleeve, that none of his blood should know him; for, or then, we nor none of us all never knew that ever he bare token or sign of maid, lady, ne gentlewoman. Fie on him, said the queen, yet for all his pride and boasting, there ye proved yourself his better. Nay, madam, say ye never more so, for he beat me and my fellows, and might have slain us, an he had would. Fie on him, said the queen, for I heard Sir Gawaine say before my lord Arthur, that] it were marvel to tell the great love that is between the fair maiden of Astolat and him. Madam, said Sir Bors, I may not warn Sir Gawaine to say what it pleased him: but I dare say as for my lord Sir Launcelot, that he loveth no lady, gentlewoman, nor maid, but all he loveth in like much, and therefore, madam, said Sir Bors, ye may say what ye will, but wit ye well I will haste me to seek him, and find him wheresoever he be, and God send me good tidings of him. And so leave we them there, and speak we of Sir Launcelot, that lay in great peril.

" So as fair Elaine came to Winchester, she sought there all about, and by fortune Sir Lavaine was ridden to play him, to enchafe his horse. And anon as Elaine saw him she knew him, and then she cried onloud until him. And when he heard her, anon he came to her; and then she asked her brother, How did my lord, Sir Launcelot? Who told you, sister, that my lord's name was Sir Launcelot? Then she told him how Sir Gawaine by his shield knew him. So they rode together till that they came to the hermitage, and anon she alight. So Sir Lavaine brought her in to Sir Launcelot. And when she saw him lie so sick and pale in his bed, she might not speak, but suddenly she fell to the earth down suddenly in a swoon, and there she lay a great while. And when she was relieved she sighed, and said, My lord Sir Launcelot, alas, why be ye in this plight? and then she swooned again. And then Sir Launcelot prayed Sir Lavaine to take her up,—And bring her to me. And when she came to herself, Sir Launcelot kissed her, and said, Fair maiden, why fare ye thus? Ye put me to pain; wherefore make ye no more such cheer, for, an ye be come to comfort me, ye be right welcome, and of this little hurt that I have, I shall be right hastily whole, by the grace of God. But I marvel, said Sir Launcelot, who told you my name. Then the fair maiden told him all how Sir Gawaine was lodged with her father,—And there by your shield he discovered your name. Alas, said Sir Launcelot, that me repenteth, that my name is known, for I am sure it will turn unto anger. And then Sir Launcelot compassed in his mind that Sir Gawaine would tell queen Guenever how he bare the red sleeve, and for whom, that he wist well would turn unto great anger. So this maiden, Elaine, never went from Sir Launcelot, but watched him day and night, and did such attendance to him that the French book saith there was never woman did more kindlier for man than she. Then Sir Launcelot prayed Sir Lavaine to make espies in Winchester, for Sir Bors if he came there, and told him by what tokens he should know him, by a wound in his forehead: For well I am sure, said Sir Launcelot, that Sir Bors will seek me, for he is the same good knight that hurt me.

"Now turn we unto Sir Bors de Ganis, that came unto Winchester to seek after his cousin, Sir Launcelot; and so when he came to Winchester, anon there were men that Sir Lavaine had made to lie in a watch for such a man; and anon Sir Lavaine had warning; and then Sir Lavaine came to Winchester, and found Sir Bors, and there he told him what he was, and with whom he was, and what was his name. Now, fair knight, said Sir Bors, I require you that ye will bring me to my lord Sir Launcelot. Sir, said Lavaine, take your horse, and within this hour ye shall see him. And so they departed, and came to the hermitage.

"And when Sir Bors saw Sir Launcelot lie in his bed, pale and discoloured, anon Sir Bors lost his countenance, and for kindness and pity he might not speak, but wept tenderly a great while. And then when he might speak

he said thus: O my lord Sir Launcelot, God you bless,
and send you hasty recovery; and full heavy am I of
my misfortune and of mine unhappiness, for now I may
call myself unhappy, and I dread me that God is greatly
displeased with me, that he would suffer me to have
such a shame for to hurt you, that are all our leader
and all our worship, and therefore I call myself unhappy. Alas, that ever such a caitiff knight as I am
should have power by unhappiness to hurt the most
noblest knight of the world. Where I so shamefully
set upon you and overcharged you, and where ye might
have slain me, ye saved me, and so did not I: for I,
and your blood, did to you our utterance. I marvel,
said Sir Bors, that my heart or my blood would serve
me, wherefore my lord Sir Launcelot, I ask your mercy.
Fair cousin, said Sir Launcelot, ye be right welcome,
and wit ye well overmuch ye say for to please me, the
which pleaseth me not; for why? I have the same
sought, for I would with pride have overcome you all,
and there in my pride I was near slain, and that was in
mine own default, for I might have given you warning
of my being there. And then had I had no hurt; for it
is an old said saw, there is hard battle there as kin and
friends do battle either against other; there may be no
mercy, but mortal war. Therefore, fair cousin, said Sir
Launcelot, let this speech over-pass, and all shall be
welcome that God sendeth; and let us leave off this
matter, and let us speak of some rejoicing: for this that
is done may not be undone, and let us find a remedy
how soon that I may be whole. Then Sir Bors leaned
upon his bed's side, and told Sir Launcelot how the
queen was passing wroth with him, because he ware the
red sleeve at the great justs. And there Sir Bors told
him all how Sir Gawaine discovered it by your shield
that ye left with the fair maiden of Astolat. Then is the
queen wroth, said Sir Launcelot, and therefore am I
right heavy, for I deserved no wrath, for all that I did
was because that I would not be known. Right so
excused I you, said Sir Bors, but all was in vain, for she
said more largely to me than I to you now. But is
this she, said Sir Boris, that is so busy about you, that

men call the fair maiden of Astolat? She it is, said Sir
Launcelot, that by no means I cannot put from me.
Why should ye put her from you? said Sir Bors, she is a
passing fair damsel, and well beseen and well taught;
and God would, fair cousin, said Sir Bors, that ye could
love her, but as to that I may not, nor I dare not,
counsel you. But I see well, said Sir Bors, by her
diligence about you, that she loveth you entirely. That
me repenteth, said Sir Launcelot. Sir, said Sir Bors,
she is not the first that hath lost her pain upon you, and
that is the more pity. And so they talked of many more
things. And so within three days or four, Sir Launcelot
was big and strong again.

"Then Sir Bors told Sir Launcelot how there was
sworn a great tournament and justs betwixt king Arthur
and the king of Northgalis, that should be on Allhallowmass day, beside Winchester. Is that truth? said Sir
Launcelot, then shall ye abide with me still a little
while, until that I be whole, for I feel myself right big
and strong. Blessed be God, said Sir Bors. Then were
they there nigh a month together; and ever this maiden
Elaine did ever her diligent labour, night and day, unto
Sir Launcelot, that there was never child nor wife more
meeker to father and husband, than was that fair
maiden of Astolat. Wherefore Sir Bors was greatly
pleased with her. So upon a day, by the assent of Sir
Launcelot, Sir Bors and Sir Lavaine they made the
hermit to seek in woods for divers herbs. And so Sir
Launcelot made fair Elaine to gather herbs for him, to
make him a bath. In the mean while, Sir Launcelot
made him to arm him at all pieces, and there he thought
to assay his armour and his spear, for his hurt or not.
And so when he was upon his horse, he stirred him
fiercely, and the horse was passing lusty and fresh,
because he was not laboured a month before. And
then Sir Launcelot couched that spear in the rest: that
courser lept mightily when he felt the spurs; and he
that was upon him, the which was the noblest horse of
the world, strained him mightily and stably, and kept
still the spear in the rest. And therewith Sir Launcelot
strained himself so straitly, with so great force, to get

the horse forward, that the bottom of the wound brast, both within and without, and therewithal the blood came out so fiercely that he felt himself so feeble that he might not sit upon his horse. An then Sir Launcelot cried unto Sir Bors, Ah, Sir Bors, and Sir Lavaine, help, for I am come to mine end. And therewith he fell down on the one side to the earth, like a dead corpse. And then Sir Bors and Sir Lavaine came to him, with sorrow making out of measure. And so by fortune the maiden Elaine heard their mourning, and then she came thither. And when she found Sir Launcelot there armed in that place, she cried and wept as she had been wood, and then she kissed him, and did what she might to awake him. And then she rebuked her brother and Sir Bors, and called them false traitors, why they would take him out of his bed; then she cried, and said she would appeal them of his death. With this came the holy hermit, Sir Baudewin of Britanny; and when he found Sir Launcelot in that plight he said but little, but wit ye well he was wroth; and then he bade them, Let us have him in. And so they all bare him unto the hermitage, and unarmed him, and laid him in his bed, and evermore his wound bled piteously, but he stirred no limb of him. Then the knight hermit put a thing in his nose, and a little deal of water in his mouth, and then Sir Launcelot waked of his swoon, and then the hermit stanched his bleeding. And when he might speak, he asked Sir Launcelot why he put his life in jeopardy. Sir, said Sir Launcelot, because I wend I had been strong, and also Sir Bors told me that there should be at Allhallowmass a great justs betwixt king Arthur and the king of Northgalis, and therefore I thought to assay it myself, whether I might be there or not. Ah, Sir Launcelot, said the hermit, your heart and your courage will never be done until your last day, but ye shall do now by my counsel; let Sir Bors depart from you, and let him do at that tournament what he may, and by the grace of God, said the knight hermit, by that the tournament be done, and ye come hither again, Sir Launcelot shall be as whole as ye, so that he will be governed by me."

Here follows an account of a second tournament; after which Sir Bors, returning to Launcelot, finds him well and walking.

"So then they made them ready to depart from the hermit. And so upon a morn they took their horses, and Elaine le Blank with them; and when they came to Astolat, there they were well lodged, and had great cheer of Sir Bernard the old baron, and of Sir Tirre his son. And so upon the morn, when Sir Launcelot should depart, fair Elaine brought her father with her, and Sir Tirre and Sir Lavaine, and thus she said:

"My lord Sir Launcelot, now I see ye will depart, now, fair knight and courteous knight, have mercy upon me, and suffer me not to die for thy love. What would ye that I did? said Sir Launcelot. I would have you to my husband, said Elaine. Fair damsel, I thank you, said Sir Launcelot, but truly, said he, I cast me never to be wedded man. Then, fair knight, said she, will ye be my love? Jesu defend me, said Sir Launcelot, for then I rewarded to your father and your brother full evil for their great goodness. Alas, said she, then must I die for your love. Ye shall not so, said Sir Launcelot, for wit ye well, fair maiden, I might have been married an I had would, but I never applied me to be married yet. But because, fair damsel, that ye love me as ye say ye do, I will, for your good will and kindness, shew you some goodness, and that is this; that wheresoever ye will beset your heart upon some good knight that will wed you, I shall give you together a thousand pound yearly, to you and to your heirs. Thus much will I give you, fair madam, for your kindness, and always while I live to be your own knight. Of all this, said the maiden, I will none, for, but if ye will wed me, or else be my lover, wit you well, Sir Launcelot, my good days are done. Fair damsel, said Sir Launcelot, of these two things ye must pardon me. Then she shrieked shrilly, and fell down in a swoon; and then women bare her into her chamber, and there she made overmuch sorrow. And then Sir Launcelot would depart; and there he asked Sir Lavaine what he would do.

What should I do, said Sir Lavaine, but follow you, but if ye drive me from you, or command me to go from you? Then came Sir Bernard to Sir Launcelot, and said to him, I cannot see but that my daughter Elaine will die for your sake. I may not do withal, said Sir Launcelot, for that me sore repenteth; for I report me to yourself that my proffer is fair, and me repenteth, said Sir Launcelot, that she loveth me as she doth: I was never the causer of it, for I report me to your son, I early nor late proffered her bounty nor fair behests; and as for me, said Sir Launcelot, I dare do all that a good knight should do, that she is a true maiden, both for deed and for will; and I am right heavy of her distress, for she is a full fair maiden, good, and gentle, and well taught. Father, said Sir Lavaine, I dare make good she is pure and good as my lord Sir Launcelot hath said; but she doth as I do, for since I first saw my lord Sir Launcelot I could never depart from him, nor nought I will an I may follow him. Then Sir Launcelot took his leave, and so they departed, and came unto Winchester. And when Arthur wist that Sir Launcelot was come, whole and sound, the king made great joy of him, and so did Sir Gawaine, and all the knights of the Round Table except Sir Agravaine and Sir Mordred. Also queen Guenever was wood wroth with Sir Launcelot, and would by no means speak with him, but estranged herself from him, and Sir Launcelot made all the means that he might to speak with the queen, but it would not be.

"Now speak we of the fair maiden of Astolat, that made such sorrow day and night, that she never slept, eat, nor drank; and ever she made her complaint unto Sir Launcelot. So when she had thus endured a ten days, that she feebled so that she must needs pass out of this world, then she shrived her clean, and received her Creator. And ever she complained still upon Sir Launcelot. Then her ghostly father bade her leave such thoughts. Then she said, Why should I leave such thoughts? am I not an earthly woman? and all the while the breath is in my body I may complain me, for my belief is I do none offence though I love an earthly man, and I take God to my record I never loved none but Sir Launcelot du Lake, nor never shall; and a pure maiden I am for him and for all other. And since it is the sufferance of God that I shall die for the love of so noble a knight, I beseech the High Father of heaven to have mercy upon my soul, and upon mine innumerable pains that I suffered may be allegiance of part of my sins. For sweet Lord Jesu, said the fair maiden, I take thee to record, on thee I was never great offender against thy laws, but that I loved this noble knight Sir Launcelot out of measure, and of myself, good lord, I might not withstand the fervent love wherefore I have my death. And then she called her father Sir Bernard, and her brother Sir Tirre, and heartily she prayed her father that her brother might write a letter like as she did endite it; and so her father granted her. And when the letter was written word by word as she devised, then she prayed her father that she might be watched until she were dead,—And while my body is hot, let this letter be put in my right hand, and my hand bound fast with the letter until that I be cold, and let me be put in a fair bed, with all the richest clothes that I have about me, and so let my bed, and all my richest clothes be laid with me in a chariot unto the next place where Thames is, and there let me be put within a barget, and but one man with me, such as ye trust to steer me thither, and that my barget be covered with black samite, over and over. Thus, father, I beseech you, let it be done. So her father granted it her faithfully, all things should be done like as she had devised. Then her father and her brother made great dole, for, when this was done, anon she died. And so when she was dead, the corpse, and the bed, all was led the next way unto Thames, and there a man, and the corpse, and all, were put into Thames, and so the man steered the barget unto Westminster, and there he rowed a great while to and fro or any espied it.

"So by fortune king Arthur and the queen Guenever were speaking together at a window; and so as they looked into Thames, they espied this black barget, and had marvel what it meant. Then the king called Sir

Kay, and shewed it him. Sir, said Sir Kay, wit you
well there is some new tidings. Go thither, said the
king to Sir Kay, and take with you Sir Brandiles and
Agravaine, and bring me ready word what is there.
Then these three knights departed, and came to the
barget, and went in; and there they found the fairest
corpse lying in a rich bed, and a poor man sitting in
the barget's end, and no word would he speak. So
these three knights returned unto the king again, and
told him what they found. That fair corpse will I see,
said the king. And so then the king took the queen
by the hand and went thither. Then the king made the
barget to be holden fast; and then the king and the
queen entered, with certain knights with them. And
there he saw the fairest woman lie in a rich bed, covered
unto her middle with many rich clothes, and all was
of cloth of gold, and she lay as though she had smiled.
Then the queen espied a letter in her right hand, and
told it to the king. Then the king took it, and said,
Now I am sure this letter will tell what she was, and
why she is come hither. Then the king and the queen
went out of the barget, and so commanded a certain
man to wait upon the barget. And so when the king
was come within his chamber, he called many knights
about him, and said that he would wit openly what was
written within that letter. Then the king brake it, and
made a clerk to read it; and this was the intent of the
letter:—Most noble knight, Sir Launcelot, now hath
death made us two at debate for your love; I was your
lover, that men called the fair maiden of Astolat; therefore unto all ladies I make my moan; yet pray for my
soul, and bury me at the least, and offer ye my mass-
penny. This is my last request. And a clean maiden
I died, I take God to witness. Pray for my soul, Sir
Launcelot, as thou art peerless.—This was all the
substance in the letter. And when it was read, the
king, the queen, and all the knights wept for pity of
the doleful complaints. Then was Sir Launcelot sent
for. And when he was come, king Arthur made the
letter to be read to him; and when Sir Launcelot heard
it word by word, he said, My lord Arthur, wit ye well

I am right heavy of the death of this fair damsel. God knoweth I was never causer of her death by my willing, and that will I report me to her own brother; here he is, Sir Lavaine. I will not say nay, said Sir Launcelot, but that she was both fair and good, and much I was beholden unto her, but she loved me out of measure. Ye might have shewed her, said the queen, some bounty and gentleness, that might have preserved her life. Madam, said Sir Launcelot, she would none other way be answered, but that she would be my wife or else my love, and of these two I would not grant her; but I proffered her, for her good love that she showed me, a thousand pound yearly to her and to her heirs, and to wed any manner knight that she could find best to love in her heart. For, madam, said Sir Launcelot, I love not to be constrained to love; for love must arise of the heart, and not by no constraint. That is truth, said the king, and many knights: love is free in himself, and never will be bounden; for where he is bounden he loseth himself. Then said the king unto Sir Launcelot, It will be your worship that ye oversee that she be interred worshipfully. Sir, said Sir Launcelot, that shall be done as I can best devise. And so many knights went thither to behold that fair maiden. And so upon the morn she was interred richly, and Sir Launcelot offered her mass-penny, and all the knights of the Table Round that were there at that time offered with Sir Launcelot. And then the poor man went again with the barget. Then the queen sent for Sir Launcelot, and prayed him of mercy, for why she had been wroth with him causeless. This is not the first time, said Sir Launcelot, that ye have been displeased with me causeless; but, madam, ever I must suffer you, but what sorrow I endure I take no force."

It will be seen that Tennyson has invented the whole story of the diamonds, prize of the joust, which he uses with fine skill in the dramatic moment. Otherwise he follows the main lines, only enriching them here and there: Gawain in

Malory undertakes the quest and is not sent upon
it; there is no word of Gawain's love-making with
the "lily maid"; he behaves him like a courteous
knight. I need not point out how exquisitely
Tennyson has elaborated the few hints in Malory
for the figure of Elaine; nor with what fine tact he
has cut down the unnecessary tourneyings. It is
important, however, to notice first that he chooses
this occasion to suggest through the mouth of
Guinevere a contrast between the king and Lancelot; then less explicitly, a contrast between the
loyal though sinful knight and the fickleness of
Gawain; and, again by implied contrast, he shows
the shortcoming of such a passion as Guinevere's
when set against the pure devotion of Elaine.
Elaine would not have thought, we are to understand, that "the low sun makes the colour".

You have, in short, in *Elaine*, Malory's story just
as it stands in broad outline, but simplified by the
omission of endless details of tournament, everywhere profuse in Malory; by the omission of Bors,
who is a necessary figure in Malory, since all
Lancelot's kin serve him in his love no less than
in his wars, but in Tennyson's story has no place;
you have it heightened and at least pointed by a
conscious moral purpose; and you have it unquestionably embellished by the beauty of such
passages as that which describes the castle where
Elaine lives, the hermit's cave, where

> The green light from the meadows underneath
> Struck up and lived along the milky roofs;
> And in the meadows tremulous aspen-trees
> And poplars made a noise of falling showers;

or again the description of the king's dragon-
blazoned chair and garments. To these must be
added many touches of beautiful invention; for
instance, Lancelot's disclosure of himself to Lavaine

—how admirably conceived from the mere suggestion of Lavaine's words to his father: "Father, I
dare make it good that she is a clean maid as for
my lord Sir Launcelot; but she doth as I do.   For
sithence that I first saw my lord Sir Launcelot I
could never depart from him; nor nought I will
an I may follow him."

Tennyson's also is the invention of Lancelot's
"one discourtesy that he used"; and Tennyson's
also, I regret to say, the combination by which it
is Arthur who, bringing word of the red sleeve,
first wakes jealousy in Guinevere.

Altogether, whether in what is added or what
omitted, the Idyll may stand for a fair example
of Tennyson's treatment of Malory's material; except that here there is no touch upon the story of
the Grail, which, as it completes and gives meaning to Malory's whole book, so, in spite of all the
beauties of style which are lavished on the telling
it, destroys the reasonable coherence and even the
artistic sincerity of Tennyson's.

Chapter IX.

Tennyson's Dramatic Works.

The *Idylls of the King* (with the exception of
Balin and Balan) were completed in 1872.   The
poet was then in his sixty-fourth year, but in the
score of years which were still to run almost a
half of his entire works were composed and published.   And of these later harvests more than half
was dramatic poetry.   Considered in bulk his plays
make nearer a third than a quarter of his entire
work.   Considered as part of the achievement by

which he will rank among poets, I fear they are
almost a negligible quantity. They are admirable
productions, and three at least of them stood the
test of stage representation with a large measure
of success; but the same may be said of Dryden's
tragedies, and who now reads *All for Love* or *The
Indian Emperor*? Still the plays are things that
cannot be omitted in a critical study of Tennyson's
work, and in many respects they well repay attention. Three of them, however, may be dismissed
with little ceremony. *The Falcon* is a graceful trifle,
and the large style of Tennyson's blank verse hardly
fits itself to trifles; while the story in itself, pretty in
its original setting as an Italian tale, lacks human
nature — "the saving touch of saving common
sense". *The Foresters*, his last work, is what the
Elizabethans called a masque—simply a framework
which gives occasion to elaborate pageants, interspersed with songs. The fairy interlude in it is
perhaps the worse thing that Tennyson ever wrote,
and the humorous passages are terribly mechanical. By common consent of his friends Tennyson
abounded in humour, as I have observed, but except
in his Lincolnshire verses, the *Northern Farmer*
and the rest, this quality scarcely appears in his
work. As for *The Promise of May*, which was produced by Mrs. Bernard Beere at the Globe Theatre,
and gave rise to the witty saying that the poet-
laureate, after filling the world with his verse, was
now emptying the Globe with his prose, it seems
to me frankly detestable. Edgar, the wicked prig
round whom the plot turns, is at once intolerable
and incredible. That a man should seduce a girl
is not unheard of; that a man should hold opinions
which lead him to regard morality as a convention
is not unheard of; but the two are very seldom
related as cause and effect. If a man seduces a
girl, he does so in obedience to aboriginal instincts

which have very little to say to reasoning, and the most vicious prig that ever was created probably never justified such an action to himself on such grounds as Edgar produces. And then to suggest that a man, having seduced a girl and driven her from her home, should return after a few years and propose, by way of reparation, to marry her sister, trusting in a change of name and the growth of a beard to prevent recognition in a neighbourhood where he had been perfectly well known, passes the limits even of stage possibility. Edgar is a piece of pasteboard, so is the plot. A popular dramatist, according to Lord Tennyson, said, that if he had had the play for twenty minutes he would have made it the success of the season. Very likely. For starting with the prestige of Tennyson's name, he had only slightly to embellish Farmer Dobson, Dora's lover, fling Dora into his ready arms in the last act, and send Edgar off repentant and rejected; then you would at once have had a drama such as the British public delights in. But Tennyson was at heart too much of an artist for this; he did not paint his rustics in rose-water, he made them smell of the manure-heap. The adroit dramatist, to match his conventional villain, would have vamped up conventional rustics; he would have put a rose in Dobson's button-hole, and the farmer's lumpish utterance would have given place ten minutes before the curtain to a torrent of homely and moving eloquence. Tennyson handicapped himself at the start with a didactic purpose, and was led into the artistic untruth of representing as the outcome of a certain way of thought sins which spring from very different causes; the result was that when the artist in him reasserted itself and reached after nature, there was a tumble between two stools.

The Cup stands on a very different level from the pieces I have spoken of. To begin with, it contains

a very fine dramatic situation. The first act is
improbable and unreasonable enough; there is the
old convention of a man making remarks aside,
as Sinnatus does, apparently in order that the sus-
pected listener may overhear them; there is also the
conventional foolish woman, who goes to a *rendez-
vous* with a man whom she has every reason to
mistrust. The whole structure, in short, is slight
and superficial, but it is beautifully ornamented;
Camma's speech in defence of hopeless rebellions
is a triumph of eloquence:

> Sir, if a state submit
> At once, she may be blotted out at once
> And swallow'd in the conqueror's chronicle.
> Whereas in wars of freedom and defence
> The glory and grief of battle won or lost
> Solders a race together—yea—tho' they fail,
> The names of those who fought and fell are like
> A bank'd-up fire that flashes out again
> From century to century, and at last
> May lead them on to victory—I hope so—
> Like phantoms of the Gods.

And upon this structure is built a really noble and
impressive second act, where Camma in the Temple
of Artemis gives her consent to wed Synorix her
husband's slayer, and in the high solemnity before
the shrine of the Goddess, pledges him from his
own gift, the cup, in a draught of poison. As a
stage effect it is finely conceived, and every speech
of Camma's tells as it should, whether she speaks,
after the old Greek fashion, in a riddling utterance
of double meanings, or rises into a stately strain
of verse, like a prophetess inspired by the coming
doom.

> Rouse the dead altar-flame, fling in the spices,
> Nard, cinnamon, amomum, benzoin.
> Let all the air reel into a mist of odour,
> As in the midmost heart of Paradise.
> Lay down the Lydian carpets for the king.

The king should pace on purple to his bride;
And music there to greet my lord the king.

The highest point in the poetry is undoubtedly
reached by the double invocation to Artemis—goddess of birth and goddess of death—which Synorix
and Camma pronounce before the offering of the
marriage libation.

Synorix. O Thou, that dost inspire the germ with life,
The child, a thread within the house of birth,
And give him limbs, then air, and send him forth
The glory of his father—Thou whose breath
Is balmy wind to robe our hills with grass,
And kindle all our vales with myrtle-blossom,
And roll the golden oceans of our grain,
And sway the long grape-bunches of our vines,
And fill all hearts with fatness and the lust
Of plenty—make me happy in my marriage!
   Chorus (chanting).   Artemis, Artemis, hear him, Ionian Ar-
      temis!
   Camma. O Thou that slayest the babe within the womb
Or in the being born, or after slayest him
As boy or man, great Goddess, whose storm voice
Unsockets the strong oak, and rears his root
Beyond his head, and strows our fruits, and lays
Our golden grain, and runs to sea and makes it
Foam over all the fleeted wealth of kings
And peoples, hear.
Whose arrow is the plague—whose quick flash splits
The mid-sea mast, and rifts the tower to the rock,
And hurls the victor's column down with him
That crowns it, hear.
Who causest the safe earth to shudder and gape,
And gulf and flatten in her closing chasm
Domed cities, hear.
Whose lava-torrents blast and blacken a province
To a cinder, hear.
Whose winter-cataracts find a realm and leave it
A waste of rock and ruin, hear. I call thee
To make my marriage prosper to my wish!
   Chorus. Artemis, Artemis, hear her, Ephesian Artemis!
   Camma. Artemis, Artemis, hear me, Galatian Artemis!
I call on our own Goddess in our own Temple.
   Chorus. Artemis, Artemis, hear her, Galatian Artemis!

It would be hard to better that passage of verse, and indeed the scene sinks from this climax: Camma's dying speech is tame after it. Yet although they were fortunate who saw Miss Terry, then at her very best, act in the piece, *The Cup* adds nothing to Tennyson's reputation. It is a smaller achievement than any one of the better Idylls, to say nothing of the poet's greater works; and it is hardly different in kind, for here, though you have stage effect admirably managed, you have no real drama, no interplay of character. None of the figures live. The fame of Tennyson as a dramatic artist, if such fame is to be his, must rest on the three historical plays, *Queen Mary*, *Harold*, and *Becket*.

These pieces, differing widely as they do in subject, have a common character. They are dramas of England. The main interest lies not so much in the actual plot or in the characters as in their concentrated presentment of some critical period in the "rough island story". *Harold* dramatizes the contest between Norman and Saxon rather than the story of a single ruler's rise and fall. In *Queen Mary* the central theme is the duel between Rome and Lutheranism; while in *Becket* the pith and marrow of the whole action is the strife for supremacy between the temporal and the spiritual power. Tennyson mended his hand as he went on, and *Becket* is far less abstract and political than the others; but of all three it may be said that,—whereas in Shakespeare's historical plays your attention is concentrated on a group of individuals at strife or in league with one another, so that you have to stop and reflect in order to discover behind the purely human and personal forces the larger national and political movements of which they are a part— in Tennyson it is with these wider agencies that the play is primarily concerned, and you feel, as it were, incidentally grateful for a presentment of the personalities through whom they were worked out.

Queen Mary, as it was the first of these plays— it was published in 1875 and acted at the Lyceum in 1876—so it was the extremest instance of Tennyson's peculiar method.   He himself called it a "chronicle play", and the term well describes this attempt to crowd the history of a whole reign into five acts.   The dramatist is not content to fix himself upon the central theme of the play,—that conflict between Lutheran and Roman which makes the pivot of the whole history; nor upon the human motive,—Mary's barren passion for a husband to whom she is repugnant, which links itself naturally with the religious struggle, since Mary in wedding Philip deliberately gave over her whole kingdom to be the engine of Rome.   He will not omit even the side issues.   And thus we have a picture of the court intrigues and conflicts which kept Elizabeth a prisoner but saved her from the block; we have a picture of the diplomatic rivalry between France and England, and even in the end the further division of forces when Mary finds that in allying herself to Spain she is leagued with a power that makes war upon Rome.   Given the general conception, it is difficult to say how any of these elements could have been omitted; but the truth is that the conception was unsound.   A play must interest, and it is scarcely conceivable that *Queen Mary* should interest any possible audience.   It will be answered that Shakespeare wrote chronicle plays, that his audiences approved them, and that therefore if we are not a degenerate race the same things ought to please us.   But in Shakespeare's day the stage provided the public not merely with artistic excitement but with instruction.   It was an age of few books, and there is no doubt that

many a man went to see *Henry VI.* because
he wanted to know something of his country's
history.   Books of history were not many, and
they were dull, while the historical romance was
not yet dreamed of.   Shakespeare's chronicle plays
have vanished from the boards except two.   In
Richard III. the extraordinary dramatic possibilities of the subject, and the extraordinary vigour
with which they were developed, have triumphed
over the inherent defects of the form; and *Henry
IV.* is kept alive for the sake of the greatest of
all comic characters.   But in *Queen Mary* the
element of humour is entirely absent; the story,
in so far as it concerns the central figure, is
not exciting, while Mary's character is not cal-
culated to draw easy sympathy; and the mass of
material to be handled has compelled the poet to
retrench the ornamentation of which he was so
great a master.   Many of the scenes, though entirely admirable in expression, are adorned with
neither wit nor poetry; the debate where Gardiner
advocates persecution, against Pole who deprecates
it, is a fine piece of work, but the verse has not
the spring and elasticity which gives to similar
passages in Shakespeare the exhilaration of poetry.
    There are two really dramatic moments in this
succession of loosely-connected scenes, though they
do not relate themselves to each other, nor is either
vital to the existence of the drama.   The first is
the concluding scene of Wyatt's rebellion, where
the Queen and her Court wait barricaded in the
gatehouse of Westminster Palace and listen to
messenger after messenger coming in with news of
the rebels' unchecked advance.   Her counsellors
press the Queen to fly, but the Tudor blood in her
rises higher and higher as the danger grows more
imminent, and she answers at first with rebuke,
then with taunts, till suddenly the tide turns and

Wyatt's defeat is announced.   Then comes a burst
of vindictive command and wild exultation:

> My foes are at my feet, and I am Queen;

but in a moment the woman reasserts herself over
the ruler, and her cry changes to—

> My foes are at my feet, and Philip king.

Still more finely dramatic is the scene in St. Mary's
Church at Oxford—indeed both the scenes in which
Cranmer appears, for they work continuously to
the climax—where, set up on a platform to read his
final recantation before he goes to the stake, the old
man in a speech full of superb poetry recants indeed,
but recants his recantation, declaring with his last
utterance for the Protestant faith which he had
weakly abjured.

Still, the situation here was made ready to the
artist's hand, and a lesser man could hardly have
missed it.   What is really striking and original in
this play is the character of Mary herself; the
woman in whom religious fanaticism — the cold
heat of persecuting zeal, strengthened by the im-
perious Tudor will, and exasperated by the opposi-
tion to her succession,—has blended itself inextricably with the hopeless passion of an unattractive
woman for a man eleven years younger than herself.
All emotions in her—the sovereign's desire for irresistible authority, the zealot's fervour for a faith,
the barren woman's longing for a child, and the
neglected wife's passionate eagerness to win an
answer to her love—all these reinforce each other
and give to her language and her actions that exaltation which is half sprung from over-stimulated
craving of the senses and affections, half truly
spiritual.   The speech that she utters alone when
she has fancied that she "felt the motion of her
babe" is truly lyrical, and truly natural moreover.

Mary. He hath awaked! he hath awaked!
He stirs within the darkness!
Oh, Philip, husband! now thy love to mine
Will cling more close, and those bleak manners thaw,
That make me shamed and tongue-tied in my love.
The second Prince of Peace—
The great unborn defender of the Faith,
Who will avenge me of mine enemies—
He comes, and my star rises.
The stormy Wyatts and Northumberlands,
The proud ambitions of Elizabeth,
And all her fieriest partisans—are pale
Before my star!
The light of this new learning wanes and dies:
The ghosts of Luther and Zuinglius fade
Into the deathless hell which is their doom
Before my star!
His sceptre shall go forth from Ind to Ind!
His sword shall hew the heretic peoples down!
His faith shall clothe the world that will be his,
Like universal air and sunshine! Open,
Ye everlasting gates! The King is here!—
My star, my son!

All the motions of this strong nature thwarted—its rancorous hate, its morbid fondness, its stubborn pride, and its desperate courage,—are rendered in their turn, separately or in fusion, till the woman stands out, and amid the despair of the last act she is brought visibly before us, in the scene where she takes the lute from her ladies and sings her song, which ranks high among Tennyson's lyrics.

Hapless doom ot woman happy in betrothing!
Beauty passes like a breath and love is lost in loathing:
Low, my lute; speak low, my lute, but say the world is nothing—
   Low, lute, low!

Love will hover round the flowers when they first awaken;
Love will fly the fallen leaf, and not be overtaken;
Low, my lute! oh low, my lute! we fade and are forsaken—
   Low, dear lute, low!

Take it away? not low enough for me!
 Alice. Your grace hath a low voice.

Mary.   How dare you say it?
Even for that he hates me. A low voice
Lost in a wilderness where none can hear!
A voice of shipwreck on a shoreless sea!
A low voice from the dust and from the grave.
(*Sitting on the ground.*) There, am I low enough now?
    Alice. Good Lord! how grim and ghastly looks her Grace,
With both her knees drawn upward to her chin.
There was an old-world tomb beside my father's
And this was open'd, and the dead were found
Sitting, and in this fashion; she looks a corpse.

I do not know anything in Tennyson that gives
a more vivid picture to the eye than this passage.
But that is a merit of the poet rather than of the
playwright, and from the dramatic point of view
the play, I think, would always be a failure (apart
from the *succès d'estime*), because the chief character
is essentially one to excite pity without sympathy—
an emotion much too complex to hold an audience.

Harold is in many ways a better piece of work
than *Queen Mary.* It is simpler, better knit
together, and runs more smoothly to its conclusion.
Yet somehow I should not rate it so highly as the
earlier drama. Everything in it, every action,
every speech and character, is coherent, probable,
and plausible, but neither word nor action seems
inevitable and entirely convincing. It is a question whether an artist should make his work turn
upon a motive with which he has no possible
sympathy. Certainly the action of Harold is in no
way altered by the oath which he swore to William
on the covered bones of the saints; if a curse is to
come on him, he disregards it and makes the best
headway that he can against disastrous chances.
Yet the whole atmosphere of the play is charged
with the curse; in the fine opening scene all men's
minds are full of the comet that glares over
England, a menace of divine wrath, and Harold,
the one man who disregards superstition and defies

augury, is forthwith thrown into a plight where all
the machinery of the Church is employed to play
upon a conscience, already uneasy over a promise
given with no purpose of fulfilment, and to instil into
it a dread of the supernatural.   It does not seem to
me that the half-rationalizing, half-credulous attitude which Harold is made to assume fits with the
man or the times; it reads throughout like a nine-
teenth-century comment on the beliefs of eight
centuries ago.   There is no single character in the
play drawn with the subtlety that marks the portrait
of Mary, and no scene at all so really dramatic as
Cranmer's declaration of faith on the scaffold at St.
Mary's.   Actors have, I think, shown their wisdom
in abstaining from attempts to produce *Harold*;
and there are few things in the language so nearly
excellent throughout that are so uninteresting to
read.   The conflict of Norman and Saxon is shown,
not as the victory of a higher civilization over a
lower, but as the triumph of forces united under
a single will over a kingdom distracted by too
many princelings.   Tennyson is even so insular
as to imply throughout a preponderance of moral
virtues among the Saxons; the libertine Normans
are coming to debauch the modest women of
England.   This is carrying the habit of British
self-righteousness an amazingly long way back.

There remains to be considered the last, and in
my opinion by far the best of these plays, the
drama of *Becket*.   Here you have a great theme—
the struggle of church and throne for supremacy—
put into terms of human passion; for it is really
a long duel of two personalities, Becket's and
Henry's, each using all his advantages, moral and
material, to break the will of the other.   The conflict of wills is foreshadowed in the prologue, where
the king and his chancellor face each other over
the chess-board, and it continues to the end.   The

two men are strongly drawn; their words and actions do not seem dictated in accordance with a formula in the poet's mind, but spring from nature itself. Eleanor the Queen, too, is conceived with great subtlety of portraiture; hers is the jealousy that outlives love and finds itself allied with other passions. She hates Rosamund not because she is Henry's paramour—to that she would be indifferent — but because she has won a love which Eleanor herself never held; and she hates her too because a woman whom the king loves may be a power in the state. She hates her, moreover, because Becket protects her, and she herself would gladly find favour in Becket's eyes. Rosamund is pretty and pathetic, the scenes between her and Henry should be affecting on the stage; but it is hard to forgive the passion for propriety which made Tennyson complicate his plot with the unreasonable invention that Rosamund was ignorant of the king's marriage. To be so she must have been guileless indeed, and Tennyson writes to represent her as a woman with intelligence as well as devotion, who has sacrificed her maiden honour with her eyes open for the sake of the man she loves. And it is no ignorant girl that turns thus upon the Queen at the threat of death:

> And I will fly with my sweet boy to heaven,
> And shriek to all the saints among the stars:
> "Eleanor of Aquitaine, Eleanor of England!
> Murder'd by that adulteress Eleanor,
> Whose doings are a horror to the east,
> A hissing in the west!"

But the strength of the play lies in the characters of Becket and the King, each admirably rendered. Nothing shows Tennyson's religious bias more strongly than the persistency with which he enlists our sympathy for Henry's side of the argument.

The case for secular control of the clerics is put
at its very strongest, the answer is left on a merely
theological ground:

> Shall hands that do create the Lord be bound
> Behind the back like laymen-criminals?

Intensely English as Tennyson is, he is even more
intensely anti-Roman; and the cause which Becket
defended was the claim of a foreign power to interfere in our national affairs, and of the priest to be
supreme in all matters relating to conduct. Yet
while his sympathies are against the cause of Becket,
he is in love with the large humanity of the man.
This tonsured layman, suddenly promoted to an
archbishopric, has little of the priest about him.
He sighs for wife and child:

> The more or less of daily labour done,—
> The pretty gaping bills in the home-nest
> Piping for bread—the daily want supplied—
> The daily pleasure to supply it.

And more openly still, when the cloud of murder
hovers near over him—for, says he,

> The drowning man, they say, remembers all
> The chances of his life, just ere he dies—

he speaks his mind, saying to John of Salisbury—

> how much we lose, we celibates,
> Lacking the love of woman and of child,

and recalls the memory of a "little fair-haired
Norman maid", who till she died of leprosy was
"the world's lily", as Rosamund is the world's
rose. These are scarcely the touches that a poet
of Becket's church would use to paint the canonized
martyr; and perhaps a devout Catholic would hold
that Tennyson's Becket allied the question of the

church's supremacy too much with the triumph of
his individual will.   The beatitude of the meek is
not for him.   One has to deplore that the drama
is not accomplished without a mere mechanical
ingenuity that connects Rosamund with the death
of Becket.   Eleanor in the play uses the circumstance that the Archbishop has ordered her into
a nunnery to goad the king into his final fury.   It
is a clever arrangement, but a great deal too clever:
the invention is false artistically, for the murder
of Becket was a logical outcome of the king's
resentment, and needed no such adventitious circumstance to produce it.   Still, the play is a noble
piece of work, and full of beautiful lines and stately
speeches.   I need only quote:

> Prate not of bonds, for never, oh! never again
> *Shall the waste voice of the bond-breaking sea*
> Divide me from the mother church of England.

But when all is said, I question whether even
Becket will hold the stage.   It is neither good
enough nor bad enough.   The tragedies that last
may be counted on the fingers, and among the
wreckage of the Elizabethans and the poets of Ben
Jonson's day, there are many far more poignant,
though few statelier than this.   The lyrical gift upon
which I think Tennyson's fame will rest finds no
scope in the drama; and his plays for some reason
never had any of that peculiar appositeness in
thought, which gave even to his less interesting
poems so extraordinary a vogue in their own
generation.

Chapter X.

Style and Metre.

What exactly is meant by style? That is a question as old as criticism, and one which every critic has to answer for himself. Broadly speaking, it means the individual manner of doing things. If a man does any given thing often enough, from writing with a pen to bowling at cricket, he develops a way of doing it, not unlike that of other people, but distinguishable as his, and indeed inseparable from himself, stamped with the impress of his own particular endowment. This manner varies by excess or defect; it may arrive at perfect grace, it may be a contortion; but it is always there, and the more difficult the achievement, the greater will be the individual differences. Now it stands to reason that you cannot define style; a quality of this sort eludes definition. You may define the action of bowling, but you cannot define the action of a famous bowler, though you may attribute to it certain characteristics, in short, describe it: but it is highly improbable that your description will convey anything to a person who has not seen what you are describing. Still, description may help to concentrate attention upon the peculiar excellences of performance. But the difficulty of writing of Tennyson's style is that every manner results from a sort of compromise between individual endowment and imitation of a model; and we are conscious, only to a certain extent, of the peculiarities of that style which we take as our model. No man knows how he looks to others; and to a certain extent he sees his model as he sees himself. We are all bound to Tennyson by too many links of discipleship to see him clearly

and in detachment.   Dickens, for instance, and
Carlyle are as plain to us in their separate identities
as Fielding and Johnson.   We can sit and judge
of their procedure, seeing it with the senses of a
stranger: but Tennyson is still by far too near
us; and in this chapter I shall keep as closely as
possible to those formal qualities of style about
which there can be little divergence of opinion.

Nothing more need be said about his dramatic
work, for critical opinion is practically agreed that
they do not show Tennyson at his best.   It is also
probable that posterity will let them fall into as
complete oblivion as has overtaken *The Borderers*
and *Remorse*.   We have to consider him, then, as
a lyrical and narrative poet; that is to say, as a
man using language and metre either to tell a
story, to express a feeling or passion, or to set out
a train of thought.   And first, on the question of
construction, which is at least akin to that of style,
nobody can lay down the procedure of a lyric.   In
narrative there are well-recognized laws.   It is
worth noting perhaps that in the earlier narrative
poems he tends to begin at the beginning, with—

> Sir Aylmer Aylmer, that almighty man,

or—

> A prince I was, blue-eyed and fair of face;

but in the *Idylls* he adopts as a rule the more elaborate method of starting with a scene somewhere
in the middle of the story, such, for instance,
as Enid's lament over the inaction of Geraint,
which, half overheard, leads to his jealousy; and
then, after bringing this strongly before the mind's
eye, harks back to an explanation.   And it cannot
be questioned that Tennyson was a master of this
art of narrative.   *The Lover's Tale*, so strangely
incoherent when contrasted with its mature sequel,

The Golden Supper, affords an easy means to judge by what labour he arrived at this perfection. Each one of the *Idylls* is a model of story-telling; they are perfectly lucid, they hold the attention, and they never fail of such an ending as Tennyson himself preferred, where the emotion roused softens gradually away to the quiet end with the ceasing of the narrator's voice. One may or may not care for the stories; but there is no doubt that they are admirably told, so far as concerns the sequence and marshalling of events and the selection of incidents.

Excellent they are also in what is more purely a matter of style; the choice of key in which to set the recital. *Elaine* is studiously simple, *Gareth and Lynette* is elaborately pretty; in *The Holy Grail* the style feels the exaltation of the subject, and breaks into long and passionate rhapsodies of declamation; and in *The Passing of Arthur* there is the solemnity of an organ-music. But here we strike a question which reaches wider than the mere business of narrative, and concerns the architecture of all poetry. A poet working by means of language and metre has first of all to choose the tone of treatment for his subject; and from this more general choice follow consequences that dictate in all matters of detail. For instance, compare the light-hearted tone of *Hervé Riel* with the dignity of *The Revenge*: any one can see that Browning is justified by his attitude towards the subject in the use of phrases which would be incongruous in Tennyson. Given the subject, there remains a choice of language in which to express it. Given Tennyson's attitude towards the story of Lancelot and the maiden's sleeve—which is very different from Malory's—it follows that here is no place for such sonorities of diction and splendour of phrase as may rightly adorn the legend of *The Holy Grail*. Given again his attitude towards the story of Maud and her lover—that is, dramatic recital by a speaker half unhinged in mind—it is fit that the utterance should be strained and violent. Few poets, if any, have a wider range over the vocabulary; none are more discreet in their use of it.

The same holds of metre; the poet, once given his subject, has not only to select his metre appropriately, but to make the metre chosen obey the mood. And in the lyrics, need it be pointed out how admirably Tennyson fits his metre to all cadences of the emotion? Witness, of course, *Maud*; witness his ballad of *The Revenge*, where the verse moves fast or slow at will, and where short lines are introduced, either to express the hurry of an instant decision—

> Shall we fight or shall we fly?
>   Good Sir Richard, tell us now,
> For to fight is but to die;

or with equal skill to suggest the voice pausing upon words of heavy emphasis—

> We have fought such a fight for a day and a night
> As may never be fought again!
> We have won great glory, my men!
>   And a day less or more
>   At sea or ashore,
> We die—does it matter when?

A passage like that keeps through the harmony of metre all the natural rhythms of speech; and it is above all in this particular excellence—in the consummate mastery of metre—that Tennyson seems to me so great an artist.

Yet he is hardly less, if less at all, as an artist in language. The first quality of style, whether in prose or verse, to be aimed at is, I think, lucidity. Contemporary opinion is against me in this matter, and critics are apt to set little store by the pains which a man takes to be understood; but clearness seldom fails of its ultimate reward. Tennyson, as I have pointed out in an earlier chapter, was at first freely accused of obscurity; and it must be allowed that certain passages of *In Memoriam* are very difficult to follow. But not all thoughts admit of equal clearness in exposition, and the thought in these passages is of necessity complex. *Maud* puzzled the critics greatly at its first appearance; it is not easy to see why, as a very little imagination supplies easily the necessary links.[1] But for the most part it will be conceded that Tennyson had a singular power of expressing ideas, even complex ideas, so that the thought should be lucid and harmonious. Yet this gift of lucidity, though it stands first, is not the highest of a poet. The highest, if we are to exclude the dramatic power to make a living man put his whole self into a word, is the quality of magical suggestion. Literature affords no better instance than Virgil's

> Sunt lacrimae rerum et mentem mortalia tangunt.

This is something even higher than the Horatian felicity of expression which packs a definite thought into words that become inseparable from it, like the *Rectius vives* Ode: yet in Horace too you can match it with a passage—

> Nos ubi decidimus
> Quo pater Aeneas, quo dives Tullus et Ancus,
> Pulvis et umbra sumus.

Lines like these can never be adequately translated. Virgil's line can scarcely be translated at all, it can only be felt; it has the magic of Shakespeare. That

---

[1] As an instance, Lewis Carroll (*Life*, p. 71) was so slow of comprehension as to need an explanation from Tennyson of "Well, if it prove a girl, my boy will have plenty; so let it be".

is where one cannot be sure about a contemporary. Will any lines in Tennyson have this magical suggestion, this imperishable accent? I seem to hear it in *Ulysses*, I seem to hear it in *Tears, idle tears*, I seem to hear it in the germinal lines of *Maud*.

> Oh that 'twere possible,
>   After long quiet and pain,
> To find the arms of my true love
>   Round me once again!

Where do the words come from? we ask ourselves over lines like these: what is there in them that should stir vague hopes and long-forgotten regrets and set all the vaults of our memory echoing? If we had the answer, we should be able to define poetry.

This is the highest thing in poetry, this power of intellectual suggestion beyond the thought actually put into words. Quite different from it is the mere quotable felicity of language like the lines on Lancelot's "honour rooted in dishonour": quite different again is the quality of sense-suggestion, on which I have dwelt in regard to landscape. Both of these gifts Tennyson had to perfection, and especially the latter. No man ever had a greater power of setting the eye to work through the brain; and this depends, first, on a marvellously close observation; secondly, on that power of selection which is so essential to the artist. Tennyson knows in an instant the value of a touch like—

> The rooks are blown about the sky.

And further, it depends upon a dexterity in the use of words which has never been surpassed. Tennyson can do anything with words. He can paint you a Dutch picture of still life, like his pie—

> Where quail and pigeon, lark and leveret lay
> Embedded and enjellied:

that instantly brings the thing before your eyes, and, as a fabric of words, is in itself a masterpiece of technical skill; or he can show you the dog at work who—

> With inward yelp and restless forefoot plies
> His function of the woodland.

He knows, too, no man better, the value of that perpetual slight novelty, which Aristotle writes of, and he keeps the mind continually awake by the use of some epithet slightly diverted from its habitual application, gaining or lending a new beauty. The thing is nowhere better exemplified than in the line which at once praises Virgil for this particular gift and illustrates it:

All the charm of all the Muses often flowering in a *lonely* word.

Yet, like Virgil, he seldom parades his graces; he seldom deviates into extravagance. Exception must be made for passages like the opening and close of *Maud*, where one sees certain qualities of his style carrried to an excess; but the typical style of Tennyson must remain always, I think, among the most graceful and sanest of our English poetic manners. It is extremely original; in fifty years perhaps men will see it distinctly enough to trace its affinities better; yet even in the *Poems by Two Brothers* there are these lines which suggest to my mind no poet but Alfred Tennyson:

> A wan dull lengthened sheet of swimming light
> Lies the broad lake.
> . . . .
> Beneath, the gurgling eddies slowly creep
> Blackened by foliage, and the glutting wave,
> That saps eternally the cold grey steep,
> Sounds heavily within the hollow cave.

There you have a very early example, and a very

complete one, first, of the landscape effects in which
Tennyson always excelled; and, secondly, of that
device which he carried perhaps further than any
other poet has ever done—perhaps indeed too far—
the suggestion of sound.

This is, strictly speaking, a trick of language
rather than of metre; it can be done in prose just
as well as in verse; and the verse which does it
most successfully borrows from prose; for instance,
Clarence Mangan's grim refrain:

> I heard four planks
> Fall down with a hollow echo.

But Tennyson used it incessantly as an aid to the
effect of metre. Metre is a device natural to man
to express emotion. Man has sung as long as the
birds, and he has always rendered the quickening
of his pulses by some sort of rhythm. Whether in
a lyric the metre chooses the expression or the expression the metre it would not always be easy to
say. The opening line of *The Revenge*—

> At Flores in the Azores Sir Richard Grenville lay—

was in Tennyson's desk for years; the metrical inspiration of the subject came first. But in the
gradual development of art men found that they
could do a great deal with metre besides rendering
the general idea of physical exaltation, and one of
their earliest discoveries was this power of actual
physical suggestion. Many ruder artists had given
the sound of a fall in words before Virgil ended a
line with *procumbit humi bos*; and many had caught
the echo of a gallop before he wrote—

> Quadrupedante putrem sonitu quatit ungula campum.

These, of course, are flagrant instances, where
indeed the device becomes too obvious, and it is

not hard to parallel them from Tennyson, since every excellence is apt to run into excess.

And my pulses closed their gates with a shock on my heart as I
    heard
The shrill-edged shriek of a mother divide the shuddering night.

There, as elsewhere in the same poem, the overcharged alliteration heightens the effect; one may quote another bad example; listen to the thump of the pestle as the apothecary sits—

To pestle a poisoned poison behind his crimson lights.

But here is a finer and more characteristic passage, which describes the lonely man haunted by the vision of Maud's "cold and clear-cut face" till he could bear it no more:

But arose, and all by myself in my own dark garden ground,
Listening now to the tide, in its *broad-flung ship-wrecking roar*,
Now to the scream of a madden'd beach dragg'd down by the
    wave,
Walk'd in a wintry wind by a ghastly glimmer, and found
The shining daffodil dead, and Orion low in his grave.

The sound of the sea and the beach is unmistakable; but it is worth noting too how the chilly effect of the wind is attained by a studied use of thin vowel sounds. Every poet gets to know by study, and instinctively chooses, the right vowel combinations as well as the right words; you cannot write lines where the main vowels are i's and e's and u's which have, for instance, the ring of—

Charge, Chester, charge! on, Stanley, on!
Were the last words of Marmion.

Examine *The Charge of the Light Brigade*, and it will appear that nearly all the strong accents fall upon a's and o's.

All these things Tennyson knew so well that he did not have to think of them.   Like Virgil, like Victor Hugo, like all poets who are first and foremost artists in metre, he arrived at his extraordinary virtuosity by an endless making of verses, a great part of which, in Tennyson's case, were never written down (in Hugo's unhappily they all were; Tennyson's used to go up the chimney with the smoke of his pipe).   At all events his mastery was complete; the lines *Silent Voices*, composed when he was all but speechless in death, are full of subtly interlaced alliterations and vowel assonances.   He had all the artifices at command till his difficulty was to restrain too great a show of artifice; to keep alliteration, for instance, within proper bounds. Sometimes it got the better of him, and one notices the lapses; but if the text of his work be studied as a whole, it is impossible not to admire the restraint with which it is used.   The opening of *Ulysses*, for instance, almost dispenses with this more obvious assonance, and relies for that sonority, which with all its monosyllables it attains, upon a careful harmony of the vowels.   The other device, that of onomatopœia, or actual suggestion of sound, so much rarer, so much more difficult, and to the average reader so much less apparent, was one in whose employment Tennyson recognized no limit. Nine times out of ten the thing is done with exquisite judgment: here, for instance—

> Just now *the dry-tongued laurels' pattering talk*
> Seem'd her light foot along the garden walk,

where the evocation of the sound is instant and beautiful.   Or again, it is done with a subtler suggestion in the lines on *Will*:

> He seems as one whose footsteps halt,
> *Toiling in immeasurable sand.*

It is as hard to say those syllables quickly—syllables which, but for designed effect, Tennyson would never have put together—as to move the feet quickly over deep sand.

I need not quote the several passages where the music of bells is caught up, as in

> The merry, merry bells of Yule;

nor, perhaps, others like this from *Godiva*:

> The shameless noon
> Was clash'd and hammer'd from a hundred towers;

but one conspicuous instance ought not to be overlooked; the description of Sir Bedivere carrying Arthur to the barge:

> Dry clash'd his harness in the icy caves
> And barren chasms, and all to left and right
> The bare black cliff clang'd round him, as he based
> His feet on juts of slippery crag that rang
> Sharp-smitten with the dint of armed heels.

It is extraordinarily clever; the armour goes clanging down with all its echoes, the same vowel sound reverberating sharply through every line; but there is, perhaps, too much of the artifice, and it begins to seem a trick. Still, it is a trick which few men have the skill to imitate; and for a final and most elaborate example of it I would refer to the earlier parts of the Wellington Ode, where one hears first the clash of bells, then the boom of cannon, at measured intervals.

Of Tennyson's mastery in metre, considered merely as the harmony of sound, there was no doubt from his first volume. Nearly everything in the Juvenilia, whatever else may be said of them, is exquisitely musical. There is a great variety of rhythms, many of them composed almost

at random in so far as concerns the length of lines
and the recurrence of rhymes; and only a man
with the greatest perfection of ear can write verse
under these conditions and hope for salvation.
Such a poem as *Life and Thought* owes all its real
impressiveness to the delicately-managed cadences
which in the last verse suddenly swell and rise,
only to fall again sadly in the last line of all, a
melody broken short. Many of the more elaborate
devices which were subsequently caught up by
Rossetti and Morris—especially the refrain—are
traceable to this volume. Where Tennyson got
them from I do not know; the history of his early
reading would have to be written for us to answer
that question. But many things in these early
works, and some of the songs in *The Princess*,
suggest to my mind that he owed a good deal to
the example of Moore, whose skill in evoking the
more obvious harmonies out of words has been
hardly enough recognized.

The 1842 volume presented also a great but
hardly so great a variety of metres. The elaborate
quatrain of *The Palace of Art* and *The Dream of
Fair Women* was, I believe, Tennyson's own. In
The Lady of Shalott he employed with great skill
a beautiful stanza to which he never returned
except in *Sir Lancelot and Queen Guinevere*, finding, no doubt, that the exigencies of the rhyme
were too great; as it is, he strains the laws of
rhyme to comply with them, and the first edition
sinned considerably more in that respect than the
existing text. The same remark applies to the
metre of *The Two Voices*, almost the only instance
where, in my judgment, Tennyson chose a measure
ill fitted to his subject. The result is a roughness
and obscurity of expression which it would not be
easy to parallel in his other work.

In the opening of *The Lotos-Eaters*—and there

only—he employed with admirable mastery the Spenserian stanza; the chorus is composed in irregular staves of rhymed iambic lines; the length of line and disposition of the rhymes varying at the poet's will; the last strophe, which was added later, is written in what is practically the long trochaic metre of *Locksley Hall*, but used in a very different way; the cæsura much less regular, and the division into couplets ignored, while in many cases the accent is so placed as to lose the trochaic character almost entirely.

But the tendency on the whole in this volume was towards a greater sobriety of metrical effect and a more disciplined verse. Tennyson was disposed to loosen the fetters of rhyme. He had published his first essays in blank verse—*Ulysses*, *Œnone*, and the *Morte d'Arthur*; he had shown in *Day Dreams* and other poems what rich harmonies might be drawn from the old and well-known stanzas; and he had also in one or two short poems put forth the stanza of *In Memoriam*.

There has been much dispute over the genesis of this type of verse. I myself count it the easiest supposition to believe that it was the poet's own device, for the simple transposition of the commonest of all stanzas, the octosyllabic with alternate rhymes, was not a difficult invention; and once the idea occurred to so good an artist, the advantages of it were obvious, since the monotonous recurrence of rhymes is at once avoided. The ingenuity of scholars has pointed out that the octosyllabic quatrain with rhymes thus disposed occurs in Ben Jonson and Sidney. Yet in Sidney the internal rhymes are double, and the whole character of the verse is altered by this; nor is Ben Jonson's treatment of the stanza at all like what we meet in *In Memoriam*.

But Mr. Churton Collins in his edition of the

Poems of Lord Herbert of Cherbury (who died in 1648) has noted a much more striking precedent. The metre of *In Memoriam* is used by Lord Herbert in two poems, of which the first (*A Ditty*) has little merit or interest, but the second anticipates Tennyson in the most surprising way. Not only is the movement of the metre almost identical in many stanzas, but there is a correspondence in thought which, one would have thought, could hardly be accidental. Herbert's poem is called *An Ode upon a Question moved whether Love should continue for ever.* It describes two lovers, Melander and Celinda, walking in a grove in spring, and communing of love:

> When, with a sweet though troubled look,
>   She first brake silence, saying "Dear Friend,
>   O that our love might take no end
> Or never had beginning took".

And she goes on to explain that she does not fear death, but that if death had taken Melander, she would be joyful—

> To come where your loved presence is.

Her fear is that love may not last beyond death:

> Only if love's fire with the breath
>   Of life be kindléd, I doubt
>   With our last air 'twill be breathed out
> And quenchéd with the cold of death.

That is the fear expressed in many different ways by Tennyson in *In Memoriam.* Melander answers in stanzas that at every other verse recall Tennyson's line of thought, though they are based upon a literal acceptance of the Church's doctrines. Shall evil desires last, he asks, and suffer their punishment in hell—

And shall our Love, so far beyond
    That low and dying appetite,
    And which so chaste desires unite,
Not hold in an eternal bond?

No, he answers; if the evil lasts so must the goodness of pure love:

Else were our souls in vain elect,
    And vainer yet were Heaven's laws,
    When to an everlasting Cause
They gave a perishing Effect.

  .   .   .   .   .   .

These eyes again, then, eyes shall see,
    And hands again these hands enfold,
    And all chaste pleasures can be told
Shall with us everlasting be.

For if no use of sense remain
    When bodies once this life forsake,
    Or could they no delight partake,
Why should they ever rise again?

And if every imperfect mind
    Make love the end of knowledge here,
    How perfect will our love be where
All imperfection is refined!

  .   .   .   .   .   .

So when from hence we shall be gone,
    And be no more nor you nor I,
    As one another's mystery
Each shall be both, yet both but one.

I have italicised a few lines, but the resemblance is
everywhere so striking, both in the thought and the
fall of the verse, that nothing short of a positive
assurance that Tennyson had not read the poem
would make me question that Herbert suggested to
him the metre.

    This assurance, however, is given in the *Life*.
Tennyson never read Lord Herbert's poem till
1880. Moreover, there is no doubt that the verse
itself very largely determines the use of it: that
anyone writing in the stanza of *In Memoriam* would

write more or less like Tennyson. This may be
fairly inferred from a very odd resemblance which
an ingenious and widely-read friend has pointed out
to me.   In 1806 was published an anthology called
The Lyre of Love, edited, according to the catalogue
in the British Museum, by P. L. Courtier.   It
included selections from Surrey, Wyat, and from
many of the Elizabethan and Cavalier poets who
were then but little known; coming down to modern
times, it included a good deal of trash from the
magazines, among which were several poems by
P. L. Courtier, with a biographical memoir pre-
fixed, a very pretty example of puffery.   There was
also at the end a whole series of Poems entitled
Amoretta: By the Editor, who did not openly avow
his identity with P. L. Courtier.   Among them
occurs the following effusion in two stanzas:

> I wonder if her heart be still
>   The same that once I fondly met?
>   Will she her plighted faith forget?
> Or she my dearest hopes fulfil?
>
> I fear to pen the wish'd request,
>   To ask if all within be so—
>   I almost dread the truth to know,
> So changeful seems the human breast.

If the second of these stanzas were read to any
critic, he would be prepared to swear that it was
written either by Tennyson in a moment of im-
becility, or by some one with an ear for metre and
no eye for sense who was imitating *In Memoriam*.
The stanza appears naturally to lend itself either
to reflective writing or to writing which has the
appearance of reflection; the movement can never
be rapid with this particular arrangement of rhymes;
as indeed is shown sufficiently by the opening quatrain of the Miltonic or Italian sonnet.
    It is, however, quite possible that Tennyson may

have read Courtier's stanzas quoted above, and noted the possibilities of the metre, and the seed thus sown may have germinated after many years, by a process of which the poet himself was wholly unconscious.

The stanza thus added to the stock of metres well established in the language was in no sense revolutionary. But the volume in which came *Maud* marked an entirely new departure, upon which I will quote the excellent contemporary comment of *The Edinburgh Review* (Oct. 1835), written, I am told, by Mr. Coventry Patmore.

"The striking metrical novelties of this volume call for one or two remarks. In the greater portion of the principal poem we have the Anglo-Saxon principle of isochronous bars, of which the filling-up is left to the will of the poet. Hitherto all poets since the total disuse of the Anglo-Saxon measure, which long survived the Anglo-Saxon language,[1] have held themselves bound by certain classical laws fixing the invariable use or at least the great preponderance of one and the same kind of 'foot' in the same kind of verse. Coleridge in *Christabel* was the first to make a systematic attempt to regulate his verse simply by equidistant accents. In his preface to that poem he seems to regard this idea as a discovery of his own; whereas it was merely a return to the original principle of English verse. But Coleridge's practice was not by any means a full development of the principle; for throughout *Christabel* it will be found that, in each considerable passage, there is a preponderance of a particular foot, conferring on that passage a 'dactylic', 'trochaic', 'iambic', or 'anapaestic' character, as the case may be. But in the greater part of *Maud* there is really no other metrical foundation than equality of the number of accents in each verse."

[1] *Piers Plowman* was written between 1362 and 1377. The system of marking rhythm by beats rather than by syllables may be seen in the poems of Skelton who lived from 1460 to 1529.

The reviewer goes on to describe the metre as "for the most part a hexameter of the most lawless kind", recalling the hexametrical character of the old Anglo-Saxon and Icelandic verse.   There are, however, he continues, certain differences:—

"Mr. Tennyson's metre employs rhyme, which the Anglo-Saxon did not; and it does not make any systematic use of alliteration, which was essential to the Anglo-Saxon.   But these differences are not fundamental, though they may seem so at first.   Rhyme in the greater portion of *Maud* has no metrical value; and that Mr. Tennyson felt this is proved by the immense intervals at which the rhymes commonly occur, and still more by the total irregularity of these intervals.   Again, it was the monosyllabic character of the Anglo-Saxon language which rendered alliteration necessary for the indication of the places of the accents; but modern English is no longer so characterized; and in a line, say of fourteen to eighteen syllables, we have seldom any difficulty about the situation of the metrical stress in any one of its six places.

"The metre of *Maud*, then, is a real metre though a very lax one.   Indeed, to the best of our recollection it has no equal in ancient or modern verse for its freedom from law.   Such freedom is always an immense disadvantage for any but the greatest masters; and if it be hard to make up, by perpetual self-control and internal law, for the defect of external bond in ordinary blank verse, which is a comparatively strict metre, how hard (might we not say how impossible?) must it be to write up to the requirements of the new hexameter of which Mr. Tennyson is the inventor.   Neither sound nor sense can reconcile us to such lines as

Now to the scream of a madden'd beach, dragg'd down by the
    wave,   ˙

or to

        The deathful grinning mouths of the fortress flames,
        The blood-red blossom of war with a heart of fire.

The reviewer goes on to note that since Cowper all poets,

"with almost the single and great exception of Coleridge, have knowingly and purposely despised and neglected the consideration of metre as an art. The consequence has been that the verse of the last half-century presents a curious series of illustrations both of extreme poverty of metre and of very high spontaneous metrical character, the last being of course in small proportion to the first."

While begging Tennyson not to be rash with innovation, he recognizes that metre may undergo a development almost as far-reaching as that which in modern times has transfigured music. He was soon justified of his prediction by the wonderful harmonies which Mr. Swinburne, treading the path that Tennyson had opened, drew from our language. And though at present poetry inclines to return to the older and more cautious ways, it is hard to say how far the example set by *Maud* may be carried. Certainly the line between prose and verse has been since then increasingly hard to draw. Stevenson and his followers have made a prose hardly less complex or less musical than verse; and many of the young poets, following the lead of Mr. Robert Bridges, aim at subtle variation of cadence which sets the old laws of scansion a good deal at defiance. The subject, however, is too technical to be pursued here. It is sufficient to say that, after *Maud*, Tennyson wrote very little that was not in a well-defined measure; though metrical experiments always had a fascination for him. His extraordinary *tours de force* with the old classical forms—alcaic, hendecasyllabic, and the rest—are famous; and of all his experiments the most triumphant is the *Boadicea* in the metre of the *Atys* of Catullus—perhaps the most difficult line to handle ever invented. These

things, however, are merely exotic, strange specimens; one may class with them his charming
stanzas that string together names of flowers for
the mere love of the sounds:

> All among the gardens, auriculas, anemones,
> Roses and lilies and Canterbury bells.

A more excellent feat, and one which might be
imitated, though only by a finished artist, is the
metre of his *Daisy*, used also in the Invitation to
F. D. Maurice. A friend points out to me that
the suggestion for this curious quatrain almost
certainly came from FitzGerald's famous Persian
measure. Here at all events is the same arrangement of rhymes with the third line blank. But
Tennyson, with a fine subtlety, lightens and
quickens the movement of that solemn metre by introducing a two-syllabled ending in the third verse,
which gives to the eight-syllabled iambic a feminine
ending, and by altering the run of the fourth
line by a dactyl somehow cunningly let in among
the iambics. Altogether it is a very dainty piece
of craftsmanship, and gives a special character to
the two exquisite poems written in it. Another invention which will scarcely be let drop is the metre
used first in *Wages*, and later, with the addition of
another member to the verse, in *Vastness*, a strange
swinging rhythm that scans only by accent. Finest
of all his occasional inventions, however, is perhaps
the long trochaic line devised for the Ode *To Virgil*,
which is simply the metre of *Locksley Hall* with one
more trochee added after the cæsura.

But the most important of all Tennyson's con-
tributions to the riches of English metre is probably
his blank verse, regenerating that metre from the
lamentable condition to which Wordsworth had
reduced it. From his earliest essays in it—from
Œnone onwards—he proved himself capable of

drawing from the measure a sustained charm which no one since Milton had achieved. The verse of Shelley's *Alastor* had, indeed, great and beautiful qualities; it had throughout a rush and flow that Tennyson only occasionally could match; but it had not the haunting quality which marks the best work in all poetry—in Shelley's as well as the rest. Shelley's blank verse, it is true, has the great merit of being built, not of lines, but of paragraphs; yet, upon analysis, this appears to be due less to an effect of art than to the breathless character of Shelley's mind and imagination. He has the qualities of his great defect. Ideas do not present themselves to him clearly; but they do not present themselves in detachment; they have always the charm of continuity. Line flows into line, thought into thought, image into image; and pauses are far between. Now Tennyson was a very definite thinker, a very clear-eyed observer, and he had a singular gift of terse expression. The result is that he tends perhaps unduly to detach his thoughts in single lines and short phrases; the long verse-paragraph is found, of course, as, for instance, in a beautiful passage at the end of *The Princess* describing the growth of love; or many times in the *Idylls*; or in so noble an example as the ten lines of *Ulysses* that begin—

There lies the port; the vessel puffs her sail.

Yet the most characteristic passages in Tennyson are those where each line is singly beautiful, a model of harmony and expression, but a unit, not a part, in the integral whole of a verse structure: for instance, these lines from *Tithonus*—

Why should a man desire in any way
To vary from the kindly race of men,
Or pass beyond the goal of ordinance
Where all should pause, as is most meet for all?

Compared with Milton, the great master in this art, he falls short in this faculty of verse architecture; falls short also in the variety of cadences which he elicits from the instrument. Here is a passage from *Paradise Regained*:

> So spake the Eternal Father, and all Heaven
> Admiring stood a space; then into hymns
> Burst forth, *and in celestial measures moved,*
> *Circling the throne and singing*, while the hand
> Sung with the voice, and this the argument :—
> "Victory and triumph to the Son of God,
> Now entering his great duel, not of arms,
> But to vanquish by wisdom hellish wiles".

Here it is noticeable, in the first place, that Milton suggests in the few words that I have italicised the stately rhythm of the dance, but, unlike Tennyson, does not carry the suggestion to any considerable length; secondly, that the choric chant of the angels assumes a character totally different from the rest of the verse. The sound of harps and voices singing is in it; though all that is done in the first line is to substitute a dactyl for the first iambus. Tennyson never contrives or never attempts to wrest the verse thus completely from its iambic character; and herein he resembles Shakespeare; it must be said also that if he lacks Milton's variety and grandeur, he avoids his frequent roughnesses. It deserves also to be noted that he has contrived to give, on occasion, a purely lyric quality to blank verse, so that his blank-verse songs (for instance, *Tears, idle tears*) distinguish themselves as lyrics from their blank-verse narrative setting.

Grace, clearness, and felicity; those seem to be the leading characteristics of Tennyson's style; harmony and expression of his verse. Other men perhaps inferior to him have contrived to give a greater impression of force; other men have suggested deeper thoughts; but none has combined so much thought with so perfect lucidity; none has been apter in the choice of the exact epithet to flash a picture on the mind; none has shown a greater skill in making the metre answer to the emotion expressed, and even suggest the physical sensation that accompanies it.

Chapter XI.

Conclusion.

What has been said of Tennyson's style is true in a more general way of his whole poetical achievement.   We are still too near to estimate justly either him or Browning.   Their fame is undoubtedly passing into that period of eclipse which almost invariably follows the waning of a great popularity—the eclipse from which Dickens has only of late emerged, and whose full shadow rests upon George Eliot.   In twenty years we shall see better, or at least we shall see how Tennyson looks to our sons.   For the moment all that one can do is to evoke other images and set them beside that one which has grown, like a face that is all our life beside us, so familiar as to be scarcely distinct.

With Chaucer there is obviously no analogy, and, I think, no comparison; if the best verdicts go for anything, Chaucer stands next after Shakespeare and Milton.   Spenser affords a better standard by which to measure our modern.   And it must be said at once that a review of this kind makes one feel the extraordinary extent and variety of Tennyson's genius.   One need not put Tennyson's lyrics into the scale as a make-weight: the *Idylls* alone will very fitly stand comparison with *The Faery*

Queen. Allegory for allegory, I prefer the *Idylls*; for the human interest of the story, for the adventure, and for the romance, Tennyson seems to me to surpass easily Spenser's swan-song of chivalry. There are unquestionably many passages of great beauty in *The Faery Queen*; but the beauty is always one that can be paralleled from the *Idylls*—the beauty of high-wrought literary workmanship, of a somewhat languid grace of style, and of a fine sense of the romantic value of landscape. Nothing could be more characteristic of Spenser than this verse:

> For round about the walls yclothed were
> With goodly arras of great majesty,
> Woven with gold and silk so close and near
> That the rich metal lurked privily,
> As faining to be hid from envious eye;
> Yet here and there and everywhere unwares
> It showed itself, and shone unwillingly,
> Like to a discoloured snake whose hidden snares
> Through the green grass his long bright burnished back declares.

Compare with that, for instance, the description of Arthur's seat at the tournaments:

> So spake Lavaine, and when they reach'd the lists
> By Camelot in the meadow, let his eyes
> Run thro' the peopled gallery which half round
> Lay like a rainbow fall'n upon the grass,
> Until they found the clear-faced King, who sat
> Robed in red samite easily to be known,
> Since to his crown the golden dragon clung,
> And down his robe the dragon writhed in gold,
> And from the carven-work behind crept
> Two dragons gilded, sloping down to make
> Arms for his chair, while all the rest of them
> Thro' knots and loops and folds innumerable
> Fled ever thro' the woodwork, till they found
> The new design wherein they lost themselves,
> Yet with all ease, so tender was the work.

I do not say that Tennyson outdoes Spenser in his

magnificence of phrasing and sensuous richness of style; I say that he equals him in this his peculiar excellence; whereas you cannot match for charm in *The Faery Queen* such a thing as the whole story of Elaine, nor for dignity and depth the passing speech of Arthur. Yet I think that in all English literature there is no genius so like Tennyson's as that of Spenser, and I would gladly call Tennyson a greater Spenser, to whose musical utterance and luxuriant imagination has been added a greater power of thought and a gift of passionate song.

What would Tennyson have been in the days of Queen Anne? it is curious to ask oneself. Would he have carried on that tradition of the academic ode which culminated for the moment in Dryden's lyrical masterpiece, *Alexander's Feast*, to be revived fifty years later by Gray—a poet whose secure immortality promises the like to Tennyson merely for his quality of literary workmanship, and for his faculty of coining the phrase that passes current on men's lips. But in a sense Tennyson's position comes nearer that of Pope than of any other poet, although no two minds in our literature were less alike. Pope entered in upon the heritage which Dryden and his contemporaries had drawn together; he found a style rough-hewn, a literary tradition established; he perfected the style, he fulfilled to the uttermost the covenant of the tradition; and, beyond and above the value of his own achievement, he set his stamp upon all poetry in this country for close upon a century. Tennyson in the same way came in upon the wake of Wordsworth and Shelley; with less of masculine vigour than Wordsworth, with less of fire and air than Shelley, he perfected their work, he carried on their tradition, and he set the standard of poetic style, so completely that, more than half a century after he first grew famous, the flood of definite imitators

flows as strong as ever, and the most considerable
poet among us,—since Mr. Swinburne has ceased to
write—Mr. Stephen Phillips, shows unmistakably
in what school he learnt.   Tennyson no more
made a revolution in literature than did Pope;
there was a literary revolution at the Restora-
tion, and another in the days of the French
Revolution; but a great epoch in English poetry
is inseparably associated with the name of Pope,
and Tennyson will almost certainly inherit the like
distinction.   Pope is a great name, but I think
Tennyson will be a greater.   What the *Essay on
Man* was to the day of Swift and Bolingbroke, the *In
Memoriam* will be to the age of Carlyle and Darwin;
it sums up the representative thought of the time.
Pope's *Essay*, brilliant as it is, seems to us nowadays scarce poetry.   I can hardly conceive that any
future generation will not hear the true lyrical note
among the meditations of *In Memoriam*.

When we come to "commit him with his peers",
who shall determine? Byron was the only poet of
the earlier generation who attained to all Tennyson's popularity; and if we compare the works on
which their vogue rested, who shall say that the
Idylls are not equal to *Childe Harold*? while *Enoch
Arden*, *Aylmer's Field*, and the rest hold their own
very well against the *Corsairs*, *Sieges of Corinth*,
Laras, and *Giaours*.   If we wish seriously to
weigh the best and most characteristic work of each,
it is easy enough to select it; but what scales can
balance *Maud* and *In Memoriam* against *Don Juan*
and *The Vision of Judgment*?   Coleridge evades
comparison.   *The Ancient Mariner* may be set
beside anything in all literature and lose none of
its glory; but that, with two fragments, constitutes
the claim of its author to immortality.   Keats died
young and left little, but of that little at least two
poems, the *Ode to a Nightingale*, and the *Ode on a*

Grecian Urn, reach a level that Tennyson never attained. About Shelley the world has yet scarcely made up its mind; but *Adonais* and many of his lyrics at all events must stand with *The Ancient Mariner* and the best work of Keats. Of Wordsworth I would only say that, as Pope is to Dryden, so is Tennyson to Wordsworth: I question whether posterity's general voice will differentiate between their excellences more clearly than it does between the two great Augustans.

There remains Browning, whom all of us love who love poetry. But when one reviews the facts, it is hard not to believe that Browning will survive only in the anthologies. To my thinking there is no more desirable immortality. I do not hope that Browning will be read as a whole by future generations—if indeed he is so read by this one. He will always be read by the few who value original thought, for Browning was essentially an original thinker. Tennyson was a thinker, as was Pope; but, like Pope, he thought rather the thoughts of his day than thoughts inseparable from himself. The fate of Browning is tied up with that of Mr. George Meredith. Posterity may be wise enough to keep them; but more probably it will lose them and never guess what it has lost. Tennyson, whatever his rank may be, is safe. Compare *Hervé Riel* with *The Revenge,* and though the comparison is unfair to Browning, it is plain at once why one immortality is safe and the other at best doubtful.

Upon the whole, the men in English literature who seem, though for very different reasons, to have affinity with Tennyson are Spenser, Gray, and Pope; and his place, one may say with confidence, will be as high as the highest of theirs. Outside this country parallels are apt to be misleading. The comparison with De Musset is a case in point; De Musset is just as typically French as Tennyson is typically English, and by dwelling on a characteristic excellence in one it is easy to point out a corresponding defect in the other.   It would indeed be a disastrous comparison to set Tennyson's plays beside the delightful *Comédies et Proverbes*, upon which, to a foreigner, De Musset's true fame seems to rest.   But if one compares what is fairly comparable, the love passages in *Maud* to me make even the famous *Nuits* look pale and artificial.   As for Victor Hugo, I only mention him to observe that, after a supremacy perhaps less disputed than Tennyson's, he is to-day spoken of with either indifference or contempt by the younger generation of Frenchmen.   Some critics still judge him sanely, and the reaction will not be long in coming.   But it is pretty certain that in ten years it will require a certain courage to praise openly *In Memoriam* or the *Idylls*.

All the more reason to be bold while we still dare.   It was the fortune or misfortune of Tennyson to be born in a country which has twice known such a flowering of poetic genius as cannot be matched out of Greece, and his rank in the hierarchy of English poets, though it be far from the first, yet sets him high in the literature of the world.   Tennyson never, at least to my mind, recalls the Greeks.   The Latins of the Augustan age he recalls at every turn, and he may have a certain similarity of fate to theirs.   Virgil, Horace, and Ovid owe their exceptional position to an accident or a privilege.   They were the spokesmen of a world empire, the chosen poets of a speech which became the language of literature and government throughout the civilized world.   Latin has fallen from its pride of place, but the halo of Rome lingers about the head of its poets.   Ovid has lost his nimbus, and it is small boldness now to rank Tennyson high above him, appealing in confirmation to a world where English will soon be as widely familiar as ever was Latin. Horace holds us, and always will hold us, with the charm of his personality; he is at once poet and essayist; under the toga of the lyrist there hides a Montaigne. For that reason he is the favourite poet of all those who do not care for poetry; he has a delightful philosophy expressed in the most quotable form. But in so far as he is a poet, I maintain that Tennyson is his equal. Who would put the "Quis desiderio sit pudor aut modus?" into comparison with any one of a dozen lyrics in the *In Memoriam*? Even the great odes of patriotism do not surpass "Love thou thy land with love far-brought", and *The Revenge*, though in a very different key, is as noble as the passage which tells how Regulus returned to Carthage, and put aside with unmoved countenance the entreaties of his kinsmen and the populace that would have blocked his way to the port. Indeed, if you judge Horace strictly as a poet, he must come after Lucretius if not after Catullus; and with either of these Tennyson or Wordsworth may assuredly take place. But the true parallel in Latin literature for Tennyson is Virgil, and there are no two poets in the world whose qualities are more resembling.

Like Virgil, Tennyson is essentially a learned poet, essentially a poet of dumb life—"landscape-lover, lord of language": the phrase fits him who wrote it as well as him of whom it was written. Take from either of them their intricate perfection of style, their sense of the beauty and life of the silent universe, and you leave them devoid of almost everything. Passion does not come direct from them; their minds are full of echoes, and they write of the battle and the fighters in borrowed accents. Tennyson, the modern, had more of the

primitive man than the classic; there is a truly
martial ardour in his *Revenge* and his *Charge of
the Light Brigade* not to be paralleled in Virgil.
But the tourneys in the *Idylls* are strangely like
the battles of the later books of the *Æneid*; admirably academic, but lacking the sweat and dust, the
passionate cries and fierce faces of the warriors.
What one remembers of those later *Æneids* is the
brotherly devotion and joint exploits of Nisus and
Euryalus; the beautiful figures of young Pallas
and young Lausus, the agony of their fathers for
them slain: what will live of the *Idylls* is the
pathos of Elaine, the tenderness of Enid, the
courtesy in arms of Lancelot.   Throughout the
narrative work of both poets the softer emotions
preponderate.   Dido might be a creation of Tennyson's, Virgil might have told the story of Elaine.
And the best work of each is to be found outside
of the *Idylls* and outside of the *Æneid.* Each
chose his subject because he felt the desire to do
something great; but for the true Virgil one will
look, not in the *Æneid*—except in such a passage
of it as the sixth book—but in the *Eclogues* and
Georgics; and for the true Tennyson, not in the
story of Arthur's wars and the tilting and knight-
errantry of his Round Table, but in the musings of
In Memoriam or the love lyrics of *Maud.*   It does
no good to strain the analogy.   But I think it will
be plain to anyone that the *Pollio*, with its pro-
phesying of the "snakeless meadow, unlaborious
earth and oarless sea"; the praise of Italy in the
second *Georgic*, and the tale of Orpheus and Eury-
dice which closes the fourth, resemble in their
high-wrought beauty the work of our Victorian
poet.   And in one thing more than another the
Roman and the Englishman are closely allied—in
their glorification of the imperial idea, their proud
faith in the mission of their race.

Therein may lie for Tennyson, as there has lain for Virgil, a strangely wide-spread fame. He does not indeed stand almost alone in the field, as Virgil did with scarcely one serious competitor; but he has had the good fortune to be the chosen prophet of his race at a period of its widest expansion; and he may, like Horace and Virgil, go to teach boys their rudiments on the banks of rivers known to him only by name.

It is rating Tennyson high indeed to put him into comparison with Virgil, and I think he sustains the comparison, though there is no doubt as to where the greater greatness lies. That imperial style compassed by Virgil—

Wielder of the stateliest measure ever moulded by the lips of man—

was not to be attained in a modern tongue by any, save perhaps by Milton. In range of thought, in single felicities of expression, in command of pathos Tennyson may at least challenge comparison; in passion he attains what Virgil never attempted; but for the supreme magic he cannot match such lines as these:

Felix qui potuit rerum cognoscere causas
Atque metus omnes et inexorabile fatum,
Subjecit pedibus, strepitumque Acherontis avari.

Tennyson was a great, Virgil was *the* great literary artist. As one may call Tennyson without extravagance a greater Spenser, it may be admitted without dispraise that he is a lesser Virgil; and if anyone resents the terms "greater" and "lesser" in such comparisons, it suffices to say that in temper and achievement he seems a sort of connecting link between these two great names—a less dreamy Spenser, and a less materially-minded Virgil.

However we rank him, all of us are indisputably in his debt. Those of us who write—and not those who write verse only, nor even only those who write—are his disciples; we have him in our blood: he is a chief part in our endowment. We owe him thanks, not only for melody of words and beauty of images; not only for opening our eyes to what is beautiful in nature and making it yet more beautiful; but because he showed to his age poetry in what seemed at first the negation of poetry, all this march of modern discovery; and because, confronted with theories which seemed to threaten man's spiritual existence, and to make of his best hopes a delusion, he did not let himself be intimidated, but chose rather to accept truth proven as necessarily good in itself, but not as necessarily concluding in itself the search for other and higher verities. And, lastly, we are grateful to the man merely for having existed. No one can read his *Life* and his works, and look at his picture, without being aware that here at least was one who in body, mind, and spirit filled up the measure of man; one who did honour to the race, and one who assures by his life and work among us that we have not yet spent our strength. Compare Spenser the Elizabethan with Tennyson the Victorian, and say which of the two is the poet of a decadence.

Index.

Akbar's Dream, 90.

Allen, Dr., the company promoter, 11.

Amoretta, P. L. Courtier's, 214.

Ancient Sage, The, 90.

"Apostles", the, 6.

Arthurian legend, 151; Prof. Maccallum on, 151; Prof. Saintsbury on, 152.

Astrophel, Sidney's, compared with Tennyson's love poems, 44, 45.

Aylmer's Field, 128, 140.

Aytoun's review of *Maud*, 33, 34.

Ballads, Tennyson's, 145.

Ballads and other Poems, 13.

Becket, 195–198.

Blackwood's Magazine reviews *Maud*, 33, 34.

Blank verse, Tennyson's, 218; compared with Shelley's, 219; Milton's, 220; Shakespeare's, 220.

Brimley, George, essay on Tennyson, 34–36.

Browning, Tennyson compared and contrasted with, 40, 55, 108, 136, 201, 225; his *Hervé Riel* inspired form of *The Revenge*, 145.

Byron, Tennyson compared with, 224.

Cambridge school of poets, 21.

Carlyle's portrait of Tennyson, 9; his opinion of *The Two Voices*, 68.

Charge of the Light Brigade, The, 12.

Classical poems, Tennyson's, 132, 133.

Coach of Death, The, 4, 23.

Coleridge, 23.

(M 686)

Complimentary verses, Tennyson's, 141, 142.

Courtier, P. L., his *Amoretta* in *In Memoriam* stanza, 214.

Crossing the Bar, 14, 94, 148.

Cup, The, 13, 186–189.

Darwin's hypothesis, 65, 70.

De Musset, Tennyson compared with, 226.

Despair, 88, 112.

Dialect poems, Tennyson's, 142–144.

Domestic poems, Tennyson's, 139, 140.

Dowden, Prof., contrasts Tennyson and Browning, 108.

Dufferin's, Lord, letter to Tennyson, 39.

Edinburgh Review discusses poetry in the 'thirties, 17–19; Tennyson, 24; reviews *Maud*, 33; on the metre of *Maud*, 215–217.

Elaine, Jowett's opinion of, 57, 58; the story from Malory, 160–182.

English dramas, Tennyson's, 189; compared with Shakespeare's, 190, 191.

English Idyls, 10, 139, 140.

Enoch Arden, 139.

Epic and Romance, 153.

Falcon, The, 13, 185.

FitzGerald, E., 5, 13, 38, 71, 218.

Foresters, The, 14, 185.

Freedom, 110.

Gardener's Daughter, The, 140.

Garibaldi, Tennyson's guest, 96.

Gladstone's admiration for the *Idylls*, 13; voyage with Tennyson, 13; denunciation of the war passages in *Maud*, 100.
Gulliver's Travels, quotation from in illustration of *Tithonus*, 134, 135.

Hallam, Arthur, 6-8.
Happy, 60-62.
Harold, 194, 195.
Herbert of Cherbury, Lord, his *Ode* in *In Memoriam* stanza, 212, 213.
Hervé Riel compared with *The Revenge*, 145, 201.
Higher Pantheism, The, 85, 86.
Horace, Tennyson compared with, 71, 142, 203, 227.
Houghton, Lord. *See* Monckton Milnes.
Hugo, Victor, compared with Tennyson, 208, 226.

Idylls of the King, 12, 13, 36, 37, 102, 132; their love-poetry, 57-60; their spirit, 107, 108; discussed, 151-184.
In Memoriam, 8, 11, 12, 68, 114, 129; discussed, 72-85; source of the stanza, 211-214.

Jebb's, Prof., opinion of *Lucretius*, 136.
Jonson's anticipation of *In Memoriam* stanza, 211.
Jowett's opinion of *Elaine*, 57, 58.

Kant's philosophy, 91, 92.
Keats, Tennyson compared with, 225.
Ker's, Prof., distinction between Epic and Romance, 153.

Lady of Shalott, The, 7, 210.
Lionel Tennyson, 14.
Locker Lampson's appreciation of Tennyson, 15.

Lockhart reviews Tennyson, 7, 27, 31.
Locksley Hall, 10, 103, 105.
Locksley Hall Sixty Years After, 14, 105, 108, 112, 113.
Lotos-Eaters, The, 7, 137, 138.
Love-poems, Tennyson's, 40-46.
Lowe's *Yew Trees* quoted on Tennyson's observation of nature, 124-126.
Lucretius, 115, 136; Jebb's opinion of, 136.

Mabinogion, 152, 155.
Maccallum, Prof., on Arthurian legend, 151.
Malory, 152, 155, 157, 158; story of Elaine from, 160-182.
Mariana, 120.
Maud, 12, 49-57, 205, 215, 216, 217.
Metre of *Maud*, 215-217.
Metrical inventions of Tennyson, 217, 218.
Milnes, Monckton (Lord Houghton), 5, 11, 24.
Milton's blank verse, 220.
Moore, Thomas, Tennyson's poetical debt to, 210.
Morris, William, poetical debt to Tennyson, 210.

North, Christopher, reviews *Poems Chiefly Lyrical*, 7.
Northern Farmer, 143, 144.

Ode on Wellington, 148, 150.
Ode to Memory, 119.
Œnone, 7, 133, 135.
Omar Khayyam, philosophy of, 71; stanza imitated by Tennyson, 218.
Ovid, Tennyson compared with, 227.

Palace of Art, The, 7.
Patmore, Coventry, on the metre of *Maud*, 215-217.
Phillips, Stephen, his *Launçelot and*

BIBLIOLIFE

Old Books Deserve a New Life
www.bibliolife.com

Did you know that you can get most of our titles in our trademark **EasyScript**™ print format? **EasyScript**™ provides readers with a larger than average typeface, for a reading experience that's easier on the eyes.

Did you know that we have an ever-growing collection of books in many languages?

Order online:
www.bibliolife.com/store

Or to exclusively browse our **EasyScript**™ collection:
www.bibliogrande.com

At BiblioLife, we aim to make knowledge more accessible by making thousands of titles available to you – quickly and affordably.

Contact us:
BiblioLife
PO Box 21206
Charleston, SC 29413

Lightning Source UK Ltd.
Milton Keynes UK
11 September 2010

159720UK00001B/17/A